zenandhorses

zenandhorses

Lessons from a Year of Riding

ingridsoren

RODALE

Published previously as *The Zen of Horseriding* by Little, Brown and Company (UK).

© 2002 by Ingrid Soren

Printed in the United States of America
Rodale Inc. makes every effort to use acid-free ∞, recycled paper ♻.

Excerpt from "Burnt Norton" in *Four Quartets* by T. S. Eliot, © 1936 by Harcourt, Inc., and renewed 1964 by T. S. Eliot, reprinted by permission of the publisher. Excerpt from "East Coker" in *Four Quartets*, © 1940 by T. S. Eliot and renewed 1968 by Esme Valerie Eliot, reprinted by permission of Harcourt, Inc.

Cover Designer: Joanna Williams
Cover Photographer: Mitch Mandel

Library of Congress Cataloging-in-Publication Data

Soren, Ingrid.
    [Zen of horseriding]
    Zen and horses : lessons from a year of riding / Ingrid Soren.
        p.   cm.
    "Published previously as The Zen of horseriding by Little, Brown and Company"—T.p. verso.
    ISBN 1–57954–548–3 hardcover
    1. Horsemanship.   2. Zen Buddhism.   I. Title.
SF309 .S66   2002
798.2—dc21   2001007022

Distributed to the book trade by St. Martin's Press

2   4   6   8   10   9   7   5   3   1   hardcover

Visit us on the Web at www.rodalestore.com,
or call us toll-free at (800) 848-4735.

WE **INSPIRE** AND **ENABLE** PEOPLE TO IMPROVE
THEIR LIVES AND THE WORLD AROUND THEM

Dedicated to the horses,
my teachers

we gaze
even at horses
this morn of snow
—Bashō

acknowledgments

With grateful acknowledgments to Professor David Cadman for his help and encouragement with early stages of the manuscript; to my sister and niece for encouraging my attempts at riding; to Tracey for her patient teaching; and thanks to Joan, Patty and Sophie, Loretta and Sarah, and the other people who made the writing of this book so enjoyable.

My thanks to Barbara Sandford Miller, Valentine Miller, and Tony Miller for permission to quote extracts from the works of Henry Miller. Grateful acknowledgments also to Faber and Faber Ltd. for giving permission to publish lines from "Burnt Norton" and "East Coker," from *Four Quartets* by T. S. Eliot.

contents

contents

zenandhorses

ONE

first ride

Henry Miller once said that a hero is a man who has conquered his fears. So watch me, wherever you are now. Perhaps I began to be a heroine when I sat on the back of a horse for the first time in my adult life. She was aptly named Dulcie, having the sweetest of temperaments and reputedly never a bad mood in her 19 years on the planet. Built like a table and standing 14.2 hands high, this sturdy Welsh cob tolerated my uneasy presence with the nobility of a gentle giant. Fearfully, I took in her wide chest, powerful shoulders, and the huge muscles of her chocolate-brown rump. Sitting astride her, I hung on with tense legs and tight hips, my shoulders and hands rigid, jaw locked, and embarked on my first hack ever across the English countryside.

We set off in the sleepy stillness of early afternoon in late August, under a windy sky. My sister rode alongside me on her pony, Tandy, a dainty creature of iron will and uncertain temper who eyed me with disdain as she picked her way along the tracks, conscious of her elegance but also of her strength. Of the two horses, she was the boss even though she was sylphlike in comparison to the bulk of Dulcie. My sister was evidently concerned about the responsibility of taking a novice out into the lanes and tracks, but gave soothing replies to my anxious questions. She showed me how to hold the reins through my fourth and fifth fingers and instructed me to push my heels down and toes up. She had removed my sunglasses gently before we set out.

"But I always wear sunglasses," I protested.

"Not a very good idea," she suggested. She didn't say why, and only later did I realize that she didn't want to mention the subject of accidents. I acquiesced. She was the expert. I was in her hands, on her horse, and she had ridden for most of her life. It's funny: We are twins, but our interests and personalities had diverged at an early age.

We turned off the quiet lane from the paddock where she kept her horses into a tunnel of green that led through to the harvest fields. As Dulcie ambled along, I touched her strong neck with a sense of wonder and privilege that this massive animal would carry me on her back, bearing my weight with no protest. Her thick mane swung loosely to the rhythmic nod of her head as she walked, a fountain of coarse brown hair with auburn and straw-colored lights in it. I inhaled her horse scent, that delicious sweetness that I would come to love. She dropped her head to stretch her neck, and switched her ears sideways. I felt myself relax a little.

A pair of swallows swooped over the field as we emerged from the green lane. I remember a splash of scarlet pimpernel in the verge. As we walked alongside a hedge up a slope, the golden stubble exhaled the smell of harvest. A distant tractor rumbled around collecting bales of straw. The strong afternoon sun bleached the reaped fields, throwing shadows of hedgerow trees over the cut wheat.

At the top of the hill, we stopped to look back. Judith asked me how I was doing. I said I thought I'd gone to heaven: Never having seen the countryside from the back of a horse before, and being an avid walker and botanist, I was in my element. All around us lay expanses of ripened crops and stubble, punctuated only by viridian trees and lines of hedges. Swaths of corn alternated with darkly plowed earth in a far field, in brushstrokes that converged at the crest of the hill. Orange-tip butterflies flickered among rust-colored spikes of dock as Dulcie feigned starvation and made for some juicy leaves hidden in the grasses.

We rode for 2 hours that day (it seemed a much shorter time), walking mostly but with a couple of trots for which Judith prepared me in advance, offering rudimentary advice about how to rise. "You're a natural," she said, at the end of the second one. Kind of her, I thought. Personally, I felt I had been bumping around in the saddle like a sack of potatoes with no control at all. Still, I appreciated her saying it.

My memories of that ride are paradoxically vague yet intense. What I do remember clearly, though, is that the next day, I thought I would never walk again. I was stiff; I was sore; I felt crippled. My sitz bones seemed to have pierced my bottom so painfully that I could only sit with care—and on something soft. I had thought I was a fit woman—an energetic walker, a yoga teacher even. I should be supple if anyone was, but riding had gotten to parts that even the most advanced asanas apparently had not. I felt as though someone had taken my legs, pulled them wide, and tried to split me up the middle.

But even this degree of discomfort did not put me off. That day in August proved to be the beginning of something that I could never have imagined for myself, because from childhood I had had a deep-seated fear of horses. Something woke up in me after that first ride, a dawning realization that the world is only a mirror of ourselves, and like Alice, I decided to walk through the looking glass.

TWO

the dragon
of fear

Judith and I rode together once or twice a month during the autumn as the year passed through Halloween into winter. Taking a carrot with me to the paddock, I would offer it on the flat of my palm (nervously at first) to Dulcie, who took it eagerly, curling back her floppy lips to pick it up, then munching methodically as she eyed me. Tentatively, I stroked the flesh-colored muzzle between her silk-soft nostrils and felt her warm breath on my hand. I rubbed the front of her head down the wide white blaze. Then she would stretch her long neck down and return to nibbling grass, her tail blowing gently in the breeze. Wild apples lay windfallen under the hedgerow bordering the field, and old-man's-beard scrambled across the berried dogwood.

the dragon of fear

Each time we went out, I had to encounter the dragon of fear that lurked behind the looking glass. Sometimes that fear was mingled with exhilaration, as one time when Dulcie cantered flat out up a grassy lane to the top of the slope. I felt the turbo of her horsepower charge up under my body as she took off. Somehow I stayed on, more by surrendering to the inevitable than by conscious skill. In spite of terrifying thoughts of imminent death, I felt the thrill of the movement, the joy of the speed, the pleasure of the horse as she let rein to her energy. She slowed into a trot as we reached the crest of the hill, blowing noisily through her nostrils. I reined her into a walk and patted her neck to thank her for stopping. My niece, Kirsty, a bright 16-year-old who was riding behind me on Tandy (whom she had ridden since she was 8), trotted up alongside and giggled when she saw my face.

"You look so frightened," she laughed as she slowed down. I could swear that Tandy drew back her upper lip in a sneer, one of her many versatile facial expressions (she had a wonderful one for "sulk" where the lower lip jutted forward.)

I mustered as much poise as I could in response to her mirth and said, "Well, so I was . . . it's only the second time I've cantered properly." I swallowed my feelings of inadequacy, wondering whether I would ever be any good at this riding game, which seemed so difficult to me and yet came so naturally to

Kirsty, and wishing that I had started in my childhood like she had. As we rode on, a fine mist began to rise off the dark furrows, obscuring the bare wood on the hill.

On another occasion the saddle slipped, mercifully just as Dulcie was slowing down out of a trot. I slid slowly round her flank and bumped to the ground. She stopped, turned to look at me out of a placid eye, her thoughts impenetrable under long lashes. Lowering her head to eat some grass, she swished her tail in what I took for irritation. I sat for a moment to recover, aware of a late afternoon sun casting shadows across the path. I got up unscathed, my dignity more damaged than my body.

Childhood memories haunted me: As long as I could remember, I had been terrified of horses—their size, their strength, flying iron hooves kicking out, huge teeth biting me. I was a dreamer brought up with three sisters among the clanging bells of a university city. I absorbed the magic of medieval streets and stone spires and loved to read about great poets and scholars who had lived within the walls of the rambling colleges. I escaped the severities of family life by finding consolation in nature, lying in long grass under gnarled apple trees or climbing into a crooked old quince tree at the edge of the woods that surrounded our house. My twin sister was more of an extrovert than I was and less into nature and books. In a nearby paddock, she kept a horse whom she lived for and rode almost daily but whom I avoided if at all feasible, always staying on the right side of the fence and as far away as possible.

There were memories of a family friend being kicked in the back; a story—possibly apocryphal—of somebody's aunt who was saved by wearing a brooch in the nape of her neck when she likewise was kicked. Memories—or were they nightmares?—of being chased by a horse across the fen at Cambridge. All of these kept their power over me, infecting me with a recurrent virus of insecurity. Yet at the same time, another part of my psyche was saying, "Risk nothing, gain nothing." Wordsworth calls it the fear that kills: This was a double paradox, since doing so could easily kill me every time I went riding.

I was only too aware of this. Everyone I told about my new passion (it was starting to take hold) told me their catastrophe stories: road accidents, jumping accidents, broken legs when the horses fell on them, accidents in the stables, crushed ribs, terrible hunting injuries to rider and horse alike, experiences with bolting horses. My doctor looked at me with resignation: "Dangerous business," he muttered and was deaf to my enthusiasm. I heard Christopher Reeve talk on the radio about the show-jumping accident that had left him paralyzed. What did I think I was doing? One thing was for sure, I was being forced to face up to fear—to the fear of death, to my vulnerability, to my mortality.

The ultimate fear. Every time I went riding, I was confronted with it in a very real way. I became familiar with the smell of fear, the constriction of the heart and the seizure of the bowels, the panic of the stomach, the tightening of the feet and the rigid toes, the stiffening of the shoulders. Many were the times after a long canter that I would feel my upper back stiff and aching the following day.

But "to fear is not to sow" goes an Asian proverb, and something was prompting me to take risks in order to reap the unknown in whatever resulted. I had come to know from the experience of the close relationship in which I was currently trapped that fear puts up walls and locks us into a private prison. But security is not our lot, it is not the lot of the human race. I decided to trust my destiny. (In any case, fate usually intervenes when you don't—it comes along and drags you by the tail.) "Leap, and the net will appear": better the impossible than the probable, I decided, and far more interesting. Henry Miller, great thinker and my favorite mentor, whose writing was influenced by Eastern teachings, said that if you have the vision and urge to undertake great tasks, then you will find in yourself the capabilities you require. Any wisdom we might acquire, he suggests, is a process of continual enrichment by entering into the fullness of life. The mastery of great things comes with the doing of trifles; well, my little voyage of discovery about horseback riding felt just as formidable as the greatest voyage must have for the greatest explorer.

I decided to keep a diary to record my experiences with horses, to reflect on their meaning for me and how I felt about them. I had always admired the philosophy of living each day as if it were the last, but now this consciousness of the thin line between life and extinction was being put to the test: out of theory into practice. Perhaps, to get the best out of life, I should live as if I were going to die tomorrow. But like almost everyone, I live as if I were immortal (in spite of evidence to the contrary). Now I was being faced with the concrete reality of that truth. Like most human beings, my need for security was centered in the physical, material world. But actually, I reflected, this was perhaps more an issue of understanding, of inner than of outer circumstance, and maybe this was why I was learning to ride, to deepen my understanding of the symbiosis of life and death.

After one ride on Dulcie I wrote in my diary:

This is my life and with it I experiment with the truth. There is no such thing as a separate "spiritual" life (how I distrust that word now that its currency is so debased by overuse). My life is my spiritual life, every moment contains every dimension. "The notion that man has a body distinct from his soul is to be expunged," said the ultimate mystic, William Blake. The only way I can hope to understand a little about life is in the flesh, by entering into life fully.

Wittgenstein said that the mystical is not how the world is, but that it is. What a profound statement for a dreamer like myself. I cannot evade the world, I can only accept it, enter it, partake of it, to understand it. Why not extend myself, however uncomfortable that might be, in order to become fully alive? I have an innate longing not to feel stifled and secure.

A coward attempts to stop the flow of life, the flow of the river. He doesn't, of course: All he succeeds in arresting is himself. Whatever we run away from, whatever we deny or despise defeats us in the end. Maybe this painful fear, and the uncomfortable experience of being a beginner, would later become a source of joy, if I kept an open mind and accepted it honestly. It was a gamble, and there was no way to predict the odds. It was a risk I was compelled to take, springing from an imperative need for the consolation of relationship in the aftermath of several years' struggle and unhappiness within a partnership. I was embattled, stifled, and cornered; desperate to come up and breathe; and longing for a deeper understanding.

the dragon of fear

That same autumn, life offered me the tool I most needed for integrating into my life whatever it was that horseback riding was to give me, even though I didn't appreciate the connection for nearly a year. A friend introduced me to a Zen Buddhist practice of meditation. I saw no link and sought none, embarking on two separate journeys as I saw them, as a beginner, an innocent, unformed by experience and uncluttered by expectation. Since Zen is firmly grounded in the real world, and its true purpose is to see things as they are and to let everything go as it goes, there was beauty in this conjunction.

Here I was, with truly a beginner's mind both in the riding and in the practice. In the beginner's mind, there are many possibilities, but in the expert's mind, there are few—this is one of the teachings. Teaching is in every moment, teaches Zen, and I was a novice taking my first steps in zazen (in sitting), but also (although I didn't see it that way at the time) in the Zen of horseback riding.

THREE

don't "try"

The new year dawned crystalline. Iced puddles shattered into shards of glass under my boots as I walked across the fields before breakfast. It was bitterly cold. A pale sun struggled through mists that hung over the frozen fields. Nobody was around: The only inhabitants of the frosted landscape were collared doves and magpies. Somewhere a dog barked. Later, riding on Dulcie with Judith, it stayed crisp and clear: a pristine beginning as we walked the cold lanes under cold crows huddled in skeleton trees. As we rode over the deserted land under a low sun, my sister suggested that I take riding lessons, perhaps because she felt the heavy responsibility of an inexperienced rider on her shoulders.

I asked around to find recommendations for a riding stable. Several of my friends were keen riders, and although we had other common interests, this one, horses, had not yet been among them. I knew that Grace, who like me was a yoga teacher, kept her gelding in a livery stable and had taken lessons from a teacher there. She was surprised and delighted at my new enthusiasm and suggested that I have lessons at Rushbrook Stables with a teacher called Pippa. Pippa, she said, was the only beginner's teacher she knew of who understood the elements of bodywork that tied into the yoga we were doing. This work is based on the teachings of Vanda Scaravelli, herself a friend of two great yoga masters from India, B. K. S. Iyengar and T. K. V. Desikachar, and also of Krishnamurti, whose ideas have influenced her approach to her practice, in which she makes a mystical connection with nature and with life. She works with gravity and lightness, and with breathing into the stretches. Grace told me how her own riding had connected with this work and that although Pippa had no direct experience of yoga, she intuitively understood the principles and translated them into her teaching.

I booked three lessons. The drive to the stables through quiet country winter lanes took a half-hour. When I arrived for my first lesson, nervous and ill-at-ease, I was informed unsmilingly that this was Pippa's day off and that I had been booked with Shirley. Disappointed, I followed her across the yard to my horse who stood ready and tacked up. He was a chestnut thoroughbred ex-racehorse no less, called PG. I greeted him and stroked his golden neck, and he looked at me with that inscrutable eye the way horses do. Breathing in his animal scent, I felt the silk of his coat under my hand. I mounted this beautiful creature with awe and was led into the school.

"Keep shoulders, hips, heels in line. Drop into your heels! Extend them down, keep your shoulders open, hold the reins as if you were carrying a pair of mugs. Move forward with the horse, although sitting back. Rise from the saddle." The instructions came thick and fast and I wondered how on earth I was expected to remember to do all these things at the same time, not unlike when you first drive a car but with the huge difference that a horse will make an unexpected movement or have a bad mood. I felt incompetent and belittled as I bounced around in the saddle unable to coordinate my body. My hands were frozen numb, and I was chilled to the bone in the raw cold. Miserably, I tucked my fingertips under the saddle to borrow warmth from the steamy heat of PG's body. Slowly they revived, but not my spirits. Shirley, a hefty bottle blonde in—I'm guessing—her mid-twenties, was short on social graces of any kind and made no attempt to encourage me. I was sick to my stomach at displaying my inadequacy to someone so many years younger than myself who had the skills that I so obviously lacked. I felt wretched and discouraged and profoundly unimportant.

My higher self said, "Probably some humiliation is good for you," recalling Taoist teaching to be unimportant and accept disgrace willingly. But my lower self said, "I never want to go back there again." I couldn't climb into my car fast enough to drive home. My legs were still shaking and my feet were blocks of ice. Worse, my self-esteem was horribly bruised. But I had booked two more lessons, with Pippa, so I steeled myself to return for the second one.

In the intervening week, I challenged myself to look at the positive: Most of us live our lives well below our full potential, and to start a steep learning curve relatively late in life will present its difficulties. But it also has advantages, not the least of which is the beginner's mind. When we played as children, we experienced things just as they were, and were totally absorbed. This is a beginner's mind: empty, free from the habits of the expert, and sees things as they are because it doesn't know any other way. It is uncluttered by the notions and concepts that encrust our experience, that build up walls that restrict and limit the free movement of the psyche: granite walls that bruise the soul. The beginner's mind is innocent and open; it goes instinctively beyond words; and it has a sense of wonder. If I could maintain this beginner's mind as I progressed in my riding, then it surely had much to teach me.

How grateful I was to encounter the wisdom of Zen as I embarked on my adventure. Zen does not attempt to transcend anything; it remains grounded in direct experience. In the freshness of the beginner's mind there is a lack of contrivance, a simplicity and directness that honors intuition and nature. There is a spirit of playfulness about it, a natural spontaneity and freedom that is expressed through paradox by the nimble intellects of the great teachers. It nourishes self-effacement and modesty and leads to an awareness of being fully present. Zen is a gentle way, and horses are gentle by nature. They are herd creatures, homers, whose survival strategy is to protect themselves by means of flight, for which they are magnificently designed with huge hearts, massive lungs, and streamlined bodies. I found it overwhelmingly touching that such a beautiful wild animal could be brought to the degree of trust where I, a clumsy beginner, could sit on its back and be carried effortlessly, so easily and gently.

On my return to Rushbrook, I was to be disappointed a second time: Pippa was out hunting, said surly Shirley as she stubbed out her cigarette. I protested weakly but nothing could be done about the fact that she wasn't there, and I had a choice to have a lesson or not to have a lesson. I had a lesson. PG was waiting patiently by the mounting block. I patted his neck and stroked his muzzle in greeting. He put his ears forward and swished his well-groomed tail. He put up with his uneasy rider with dignified tolerance, and in spite of my fears, I could admire his sleek beauty and muscled strength as we rode around the school. "Squeeze the horse forward with the calves so that your legs wrap around him. *Relax the legs.* Don't hold on with the legs! Soft seat, soft knees, soft inner legs. Relax the hips." Another tirade of advice that was useless to one whose "feel" was blocked by fear, let alone by the discomfort brought about by being told what to do by a youngster. A piercing wind was freezing my blood, but that was nothing compared to the cold hand of despair that had its tight grip around my viscera.

Later that day, I wrote in my diary:

It's said that it's through hell that you reach heaven. . . . Well, I'd better believe it. When I decided to dance with my shadow, I had no idea that I would end up wrestling with it. Still, at the very least, I feel that taking risks and experiencing fear is preferable to the safe life I could have chosen by walking a conventional path. It makes it

*my life, my difficulty and—if worse comes to worst—my
misfortune. I've always had a reckless disregard for doing the
expected thing and it's gotten me into all sorts of trouble, but at least
I will have had a life.*

The third time around, I got Pippa. She was *it*. Unlike any
of the others I had yet met at the stables, she had a ready sense
of humor with a cheeky grin. She was a slight figure with long
mouse-fair hair tied back in a ponytail, gray-blue eyes, and pale
skin. For a very young woman looking after a not-so-young
rider, she handled me beautifully. She spoke with the obliga-
tory estuary accent of her peers but she was never patronizing,
always helpful, always encouraging. Immediately, I recognized
her different way of teaching that tied in with my way of yoga.
I was thrilled. But at the end of the lesson, while I was still sitting on the lovely PG, she delivered a thunderbolt.

"Two weeks from now, we are closing the riding school."

I felt as if I had been punched in the stomach.

"What, you mean—no more lessons?"

"I'm afraid not. You see Helen, who owns the yard, is getting married again and wants to spend more time with her new
husband. She is going to concentrate mainly on dressage and
continue with the hunting side of things. The riding school
just takes up too much of her time."

don't "try"

I was gutted. I had just found the teacher I needed—and she was being pulled from under my nose. Slowly I dismounted. I had the feeling that if I didn't seize the moment, I would regret it for the rest of my life.

"Is there any chance at all that you would take me on privately?"

"Oh, I really don't know. . . ." Pippa must have seen the look on my face. "Well, I'll have a word with Helen and see if there's any chance. But the dressage school is being rebuilt for the next couple of months, you see, and we are getting rid of most of the riding-school horses, so I'm not sure what horses we would have available for you to ride anyway."

It was with a heavy heart that I returned PG to his stable. I took his bridle off and he gave me a long nuzzle. I hugged his neck trying to hold back the tears. I felt like a disappointed child. Maybe I wouldn't see him again, this beautiful thoroughbred who had initiated me into the riding school with patience and grace. I realized for the first time why people remember the names of horses they have ridden, even decades later. The relationship, however fleeting, scores a deep emotional imprint. He looked at me with big almond eyes under downward-slanting lashes. Caressing his silky chestnut head, I wiped my eyes, swallowed hard, and left the stables feeling unbearably sad.

During the week, while I was waiting for Pippa to call, I got hold of a book she had recommended, *Ride with Your Mind* by Mary Wanless. I devoured it. Everything it said fascinated me. "Arrange the spine in the 'middle place,' breathe down into your belly, engage abdominal muscles by 'bearing down,' and use your peripheral vision. The knee is the fixed point while the pelvis is sufficiently movable to go with the movement of the horse. Very little body movement is involved. Relaxed concentration gives far greater strength than forced resistance (as in martial arts). Good riders align themselves so effectively that the horse cannot disturb their alignment." Reading these words clarified the instructions I had received but failed to understand, let alone implement.

When I came to the passage saying, "The brain cannot distinguish between real and imagined performance," I had to stop and reread it. She quoted a research experiment carried out on three groups of basketball shooters. One group practiced for 20 minutes a day, the second group didn't practice at all, and the third imagined themselves practicing. At the end of 3 weeks, the first group had improved by 24 percent, the second not at all, and the third by 23 percent. It is now well-established in the field of sports psychology that mental rehearsal is a powerful way of practicing and a valuable adjunct to the real thing. I would use it.

One of my favorite instructions to yoga pupils is to say, "Let go of the 'trying.'" Trying doesn't work. It involves mental strain and too many muscles: In yoga, as on horseback, this tightness is counterproductive. This author said the same thing: "Don't *try*!" In yoga classes, I had often seen a visible difference between when I told someone to try to touch their toes and when I told them simply to touch their toes. I was going to have to practice on horseback what I preached in yoga. Use riding, she said, as personal expansion. Whatever we believe we can become, we do become. Yes, I thought. Just like yoga.

Much as I was enjoying the book, I recognized that reading was not enough. Zen teaches that we only reach reality through direct experience, not through the intellect: The world of concepts and ideas is not the world of reality. Yet this experience of reality has to be channeled through the mind, and the power of mental rehearsal indicated that an experience experienced in the mind is translated to the body: The body is the mind, and vice versa. When we have our bodies and minds in order, everything else will exist in the right place, in the right way, says Zen teaching. The "direct experience" of Zen is inextricably mental and physical; it is a total experience. "Your life is the creation of your mind," as the Buddha said.

The body always follows the mind. As far as the body is concerned, the mind represents the pathway to the experience. Otherwise, we may have the experience but miss the meaning. My mind was prepared and my impatient Sagittarian nature eager for some of this direct experience, which in any case does not react well to waiting for the phone to ring. So I decided to take action and open the next door behind the looking glass.

FOUR

"a portion of genius"

I opened the Yellow Pages and called various local riding stables. The one that came up trumps was called Sunnyfields, a mere 15-minute drive away in a village set on the edge of rolling arable farmland overlooking the gallops of a nearby stud farm. I was thrilled to hear that they had a horse suitable for a beginner. I imagined—rightly, as it turned out—that the hacking would be spectacular. I booked a lesson and drove through the deathly quiet of the February fields. The plowed earth was showing tips of brown furrows through a blanket of light snow.

Several girls were mucking out in the stable yard when I arrived. Piles of dirty straw littered the cobbles, and two horses were drinking from a stone trough at one end. As I walked in, several faces appeared over stable doors, ears pricked forward, looking at me with curiosity. One of them started waving his head violently from side to side, while his neighbor took one look and retreated, returning to chomp on his hay. Two riders mounted the stone mounting block near the entrance and clattered out of the yard together. I was assaulted by smells of leather, manure, urine, and the sweetness of horse sweat.

Nobody acknowledged my presence for what seemed like several minutes. An overweight middle-age woman, tall, with a coarse face and untidy graying hair, was ordering the stable hands around with premenstrual unpleasantness. When she decided to spot me, she mustered just about enough civility to greet me, take my money, and find a hat for me. Her name was Madge.

With, "Johnny isn't here yet. He won't be long," she returned to shouting at her stable girls.

I hung around uneasily, trying to keep my hands and feet from going numb. I was beginning to accept that riding-school people are not conversationalists. Not even polite, usually. I wondered vaguely why, but then I gave up conjecturing and talked to the horses instead, stroking their soft noses and watching chickens wander around under the legs of a family of goats that stood near the water trough. The yard was smelly, but I liked its naturalness and informality: not posh, certainly not posh.

I liked Johnny immediately. He was camp. Camp was the last thing I would ever have imagined in a riding-school instructor. Slight, dainty, and balding, he sported a lavender shirt and salmon-pink cravat. His eccentric manner and sense of humor warmed me to him and helped me loosen up. I needed to. He remarked at once on my terror. He led me to Rocky, a 16-hands dark bay with a thin face and white blaze. He was slightly bony, his coat not as lustrous as it should have been, and his eyes not altogether happy. But he seemed placid and good-natured against all the odds.

"You could trust this horse with a baby," Johnny assured me. Soon I was at ease with Rocky, and I grew very fond of him over the coming weeks: He absorbed much of my first fears, my ineptness, my inexperience, with gentle acceptance. Johnny led me past a yard of junk cars and rusty metal barrels to the schooling ring: The gate was broken at its hinge, the fencing dilapidated. The area was small, the ground covered in scruffy chippings and shavings.

After warming up, we practiced going from a trot into a canter: Johnny showed me how the outside leg nudges behind the girth, a sensitive nerve center that in effect is the control pad, while keeping the inside rein short while making the transition. To help me with rising to the trot, he suggested that I count to its rhythm.

"Remember," he said, "control with the legs and guide with the hands. But keep the hands still. The '4-inch rule' is a useful one: Keep the hands 4 inches apart, 4 inches above the saddle, and 4 inches from the body. The hands are always kept low."

We went into a canter.

"Relax the hips into the saddle and move with the movement of the horse. The hands don't move."

Mine did, of course. But I was enjoying myself. At the end of the hour, I was hot and sweaty in spite of the arctic cold. I patted Rocky on the neck and thanked him for being so good, then swung myself down. (This was about the only thing I could do with any style, having watched countless westerns and being loose in the hips after years of yoga).

"Can I book more lessons with you? That was really good."

"Yes, sure. I teach Tuesday and Wednesday afternoons."

My heart sank.

"I teach in the afternoon, too, every day except Monday. Do you ever teach in the morning?'

"No. I'm really sorry. Those are the only times that Madge employs me here."

That was that. I was facing yet another closed door. Was fate conspiring against my insane attempt to learn to ride at this late stage in my life? I resigned myself to booking Mr. B for a hack with one of the girls the following week, and drove home through the thick frost that still encrusted the trees into the late morning. Passing the village pond, I saw two ducks huddled together by the frozen rushes, immobilized by the cold.

Between the riding school episodes, I continued to ride out on Dulcie with Judith. By now I had learned how to dress for riding in cold weather: I wore thick tights and leggings under my jodhpurs and three pairs of socks under my boots, two pairs of gloves, at least four layers of sweaters and T-shirts under a thickly padded riding coat, and a wool scarf around my neck. After too many episodes of frozen feet, I bought some insulated boots that kept my toes as warm as toast.

We would snatch an hour or two on weekday afternoons between work commitments, and explore the wintry land-scapes. I would return home with photographs in my head of a drift of homing birds floating over the copse. Warming my frozen nose and earlobes back to life, I would hear the muffled clapping of wings as big birds stirred in the empty woods, and see again the fine mist rising over the fields, obscuring the bare trees against a sky colorless with cold.

My original fear eroded a little each time I rode Dulcie. I was beginning to find her presence more comforting than threatening—something I could not have imagined. I began to find with her a sense of restoration and space. This was deeply healing to me as I struggled with my issues of relationship and solitude. I loved to stroke the soft patch between her nostrils when I greeted her, always offering my hand for her to smell before I did so. She would look at me from under lowered lashes and rub her head against my coat, asking for her carrot. I loved the way she would swivel one ear back to listen to my voice as we rode along, while keeping the other focused on what was going on around her.

As my fear lifted, Dulcie relaxed and became less restless under me. It was as if my anxiety had been infectious: Physically solid and heavy as she was, her hypersensitive wiring meant that either she could read my mind or she picked up my tension through the minutest physical manifestations of which I was completely unaware. In turn I was talking to her, resting my hands on her neck, stroking it and responding to the movement of her ears in front of me as I rode. I was learning to breathe in rhythm with her gait, which calmed both of us. Her wide rump swung in leisurely fashion behind me as we walked along, her long tail swinging in response.

Her willingness to please touched me, and I was invariably moved by the beauty of her colossal body. The first time I groomed Dulcie, I felt overwhelmed by the power of the great muscles of her quarters, her heavy feet with their iron shoes and long "feathers" half-covering them, the powerful thickness of her neck. I would brush her till she shone. She gave a little snort as I finished off her long, thick mane, seeming to say, "Don't I look beautiful now?" I was learning to appreciate the innate nature of horses that responds to leadership and a firm brand of kindness, but will never be able to forget force and cruelty, which traumatize them permanently. They respond to patience and tact by becoming willing and attentive. Force them and they will fight you. "Interfering with what is natural will always cause pain," wrote Chuang-tzu.

Xenophon, who in the 5th century B.C. wrote books on hunting, horse breeding, and the art of riding and classical dressage, which are ultimate statements on horsemanship, said that "anything that is forced or misunderstood can never be beautiful." His guidelines for the correct psychological approach to handling a horse are still valid today: This from a man whose sun god, Helios, rose daily in the east in his four-horse chariot, and for whom winged Pegasus transported the thunder and lightning of Zeus across the heavens. His contemporaries did much to further the culture of man and horse. They built hippodromes for horse racing and raced horses in the first Olympic games. Meanwhile, their children were raised on the myth of Pluto carrying Persephone off to Hades in a horse-drawn chariot. Horses inhabited their imaginations as well as their daily lives, as they have in many cultures before and since. Even my friend Henry Miller was not exempt. In *Nexus* he wrote of "Gogol and the troika. . . . He was talking horses. Stallions, that's what they were. A horse travels like wind. A horse flies. A spirited horse, anyway. How would Homer have rushed the gods back and forth without those fiery steeds he made use of? . . . And the wild stallions of Gogol were still racing like the wind."

To native North Americans, horses were godlike, mysterious beings as well as best friends. Metaphorically, they represent the freedom of flying and transcending the mundane, facilitating awakening and the discovery of new horizons. Their beauty and strength inspire wholesome awe: "Without worship you shrink," wrote Peter Shaffer in his play *Equus*. On average, a full-size horse weighs a half-ton and can move at up to 40 miles per hour. Their powerful lungs were designed to achieve this speed and if laid out flat would cover 2,990 square yards, compared to the mere 107 to 170 square yards of the human lungs. The heart of a horse is huge, adapted to pump blood efficiently around the body so that he can maintain flight: It weighs around 6½ pounds. The head has a massive dental mechanism to deal with the constant herbivorous diet, and a small cranium. (A horse is designed more for feeling than thinking.) Strong, heavy muscles are packed onto the rump, and the chest is deep and wide, with a long, extended neck that maintains balance. To misquote William Blake, "When thou seest an Horse [he wrote 'Eagle'], thou seest a portion of Genius. Lift up thy head!"

FIVE

letting go

It was 10 days before Pippa phoned to say that Helen had agreed to private lessons, although it wouldn't be on PG since someone had taken him on loan. I had had my last ride on PG, but in spite of that sadness I was both relieved and overjoyed that I would be getting the teacher I wanted. I called Grace right away to tell her. We got into one of our long talks about techniques, both of riding and of yoga, which I found so valuable in those early days.

"Get the feeling that you are pushing cheese through a grater when you urge the horse forward with the legs," she said. "In dropping into the hips, you can feel the back end of the horse moving. Feel as if you are standing, not sitting, because your heels are so well down. Spring up from your heels,

34

lengthening the knees and letting go with the hips. Let your hips move with the movement."

I absorbed all this avidly, having watched Grace ride and knowing how much more experienced she was than myself, having ridden with many good teachers. Meanwhile, I was reading *The Way to Perfect Horsemanship* by the great 20th-century horseman Udo Burger, and had jotted down in my diary his axiom that "to become a good horseman one needs to be bold, agile, and relaxed. These qualities are not physical attributes, they are psychological ones."

I drove across country to the yard early on Sunday morning for my lesson. Men were felling dead trees in a thicket at the end of my lane, and the drift of smoke up into a pale aquamarine sky seemed to herald spring. Wild arum was pushing furled shoots through the banks, and buds were bursting into leaf along the hedgerows. The smell of bonfire lingered in my car. Pippa introduced me to Helen, who looked like an exception to my newly formulated riding-school rule. She had a soft face with ruddy cheeks, wavy brown hair, and a pleasant smile.

"I've put you on Fly for the time being," she said, "although someone is interested in taking her on loan. But she'll do you for the time being."

Fly and I never really hit it off. She was a sulky dark bay, half thoroughbred with skinny legs and a white star between her eyes. Her mean expression spoke of world-weariness. I guessed she had been ridden to death in riding schools throughout her life. She seemed unresponsive to the bit, probably hardened beyond feeling, and moved when she wanted to—not when I wanted her to. She had learned a bag of tricks over the years: Horses, it appears, are ultimately our psychological masters.

We started with a trot: "Keep your legs back," called Pippa from the center of the school. "Yours come forward: your toe should remain in line with the knee if you look from above, heel in line with the hip. All the movement is in the hip, and you 'stand' into the heels."

I made some unsuccessful attempts to improve my style. She told me to keep the knees out, not to grip with them, to relax and open the hips so that they would move forward and backward with the trot rather than up and down.

"The hands stay still, upper body moves forward a little, hips stay relaxed. Feel an elastic circle of reins into the hands, through the arms and into the shoulders. Remember: Guide with the hands, control with the hips and legs. Above all, let go!"

My body didn't seem to know what that meant. I told it to, but it wouldn't.

Then Pippa announced that we would have a go at cantering. I told her that I was still scared because cantering seemed so fast. She giggled. She told me to go with the movement of the horse, to open my shoulders and not to lean either backward or forward. We went into a trot. I squeezed Fly's ribs to make her go faster, but to no avail. Too subtle perhaps, I thought. I kicked. To no avail. After about 10 minutes, I was exhausted and fighting back tears. I cheered myself slightly by recalling the saying that a Zen master's life is one mistake after another (a mistake being an opportunity to learn).

Imperfection, that was it. The acceptance of imperfection is enlightenment. Aha. Finding perfection in things as they are and not as we think they should be! Finding perfect existence through imperfect existence, this is the teaching, perfection in imperfection. In my imperfections, I would find the true way of Zen. The "worst" could prove to be the most valuable because it has the most lessons to teach. Zen was teaching me to accept things as they are, however disagreeable.

Pippa was saying, "Relax into the saddle as if you're on a rocking horse. Inside leg back a couple of inches, shorten the inside rein, but be firm on the outside rein."

I tried again. Fly stayed adamantly in a trot.

"The reason she's not going," said Pippa, obviously finding it all amusing although not unkindly so, "is that you are actually telling her *not* to go! You are so scared that your body is stiff with fear, and that is the message she is picking up. It contradicts what you are telling her with your legs. Just relax."

Just relax, I thought grimly. Easier said than done when without a safety belt you expect me to fling myself to the mercy of the elements at 100 miles an hour.

I was doing too much and trying too hard. There was too much detail confusing the horse. Simplify it, I told myself, simplify. I was still near tears. Grow up, I scolded myself. You are not a child. Anyway, I thought defiantly, I don't care.

Within a nanosecond, we were in an easy canter.

I could not believe it. Fly had picked up my thought, and because I was carefree (sort of), she freed up to go into a canter. I was ecstatic. I had thrown my fear to the winds, and then found not only that I could stay on, but also that it didn't seem so fast after all, that I could move with her movement and actually enjoy myself. It was easier than trotting!

This was one life lesson of many. Letting go was what this one was about, just as in yoga. I had gone beyond the theory and put it into practice. This was better than putting my personal dragons into their cages with a year of Western psychoanalytic therapy. I was riding the dragon instead. This innocent experience of freedom, simplicity, balance, and excitement woke me up. The essence of Zen is the experience of awakening, in which reality reveals itself complete and whole.

I was awakened to the extent of my untapped potential, to the self-imposed limits of my understanding, to a glimpse of what I really am. "Hippotherapy," that's what it was, I thought gleefully. Hippotherapy was showing me the secret of Zen practice: Just to let go and be there. I had experienced for the first time the "effortless effort" of Zen.

The Buddha said (he wasn't talking about riding, but he could have been):

> *Let go in front*
> *Let go behind*
> *Let go in the middle*
> *Gone beyond existence, with a mind free everywhere.*

What I learned from that fleeting experience (I was not able to replicate it immediately) was to reconnect with how I must have done things as a child, before I "knew" anything. Because a child does something with its whole being, it surrenders completely to what is in hand; it is fearless. Now I could understand the Zen adage that a great man retains a child's mind. The qualities required for good riding were those childlike qualities of absorbed readiness, alertness, and responsiveness.

In the beginner's mind, there are no thoughts of "I have attained something", because it is too absorbed in the process to have self-centered thoughts that limit the mind. "The wise man strives to no goals, but the foolish man fetters himself," says Seng-ts'an. The beginner's mind is also the mind of compassion and thus is vast and boundless. It is when we have no thought of achievement and no thought of self that we are true beginners. In that instant those were the things I had let go of.

Zen was giving me dragon-riding lessons with its unique blend of Indian mysticism, the Taoists' love of naturalness and spontaneity, and the pragmatism and precision of the Confucian mind. Paradoxically, it dawned on me then, there was no need for me to have an "understanding" of Zen. The only "Zen" I would find on horseback would be the Zen I took with me. To do things as if I were doing them for the first time, to see familiar things as if I had never seen them before, fresh, this was the art. I challenged myself, as I progressed in the art and the skill of riding, to keep my mind open, empty, and ready, with no thought of gain or loss, of criticism or praise, and to understand "no attainment" of Zen through the medium of horsemanship. As Zen Master Dōgen put it, "Truth is ever present. It is not something to be attained. . . . Zen is simply the expression of truth; therefore, longing and striving are not true attitudes of Zen."

SIX

no destination

Slowly spring shook off the long winter, and over those weeks I hacked out on Rocky. I booked him early one morning, and two of us set out in the exhilarating freshness of April sunshine. The horses crunched their way over the pebbles of the stable driveway and out into the road, clip-clopping rhythmically over the tarmac. A group of magpies darted in and out of the hedgerow, swooping into the field and back up into the bare oak. I rode with Karen, a very tall 17-year-old who rated about halfway on the taciturn scale but who gradually defrosted over the weeks I went out with her. A well-built girl with pink cheeks who wore her dark brown hair pulled back in a ponytail, she was one of those females who lives horses. Brought up with them, she had ridden all her life, spent all her spare time in the riding school, and had a young horse of her own that she was training for show jumping. I never fathomed what she thought of me, nor did I worry about it. I was adjusting to the age difference between me and my teachers, the reverse of the norm, and learning to ignore the feeling of ignominy that it created. I was intent instead on staying in the saddle and on establishing my friendship with Rocky. He was a good horse: steady, responsive, sensible, and reliable. I am indebted to him for the confidence I slowly acquired.

We had two great canters that day, and I managed to at least think about keeping my hands still. He responded to the squeeze of the fingers when I wanted him to stop, clever horse (this instruction came as a surprise: I always imagined you had to lean back and tug hard on the reins to make a horse stand still, *Magnificent Seven*–style, but no). We stood for a few moments at the top of the lane, watching a line of cattle drift languidly across a distant field, heads down, majestic in their indifference. Rocky went for some succulent young hazel leaves, translucent in the hedge. As we rode on, I practiced what Grace had suggested, imagining pushing cheese through a grater with my calves, although to start with I found myself doing it with my heels. I experienced the lightness that comes when you drop all your weight into your heels, and you "grow" from the waist upward as if being pulled by a hair from the middle of your head. Every time I rode, I could see new connections with Zen: Today it was that the perfection of action is a total absorption in experience, when "time stands still." It is without fear and without self-consciousness and leaves you with the feeling that in a moment of experience, time does not exist. There is no attainment and no destination. The reality of that fleeting moment is that it is timeless, giving us a glimpse into reality independent of time.

I was grateful for the fact that Karen was not chattering: I could retreat to the island of my soul, focus on what was happening, and have the space to be completely attentive. My hips began to move loosely forward and backward with Rocky's rolling walk as I relaxed into the saddle. There were elusive moments when I felt the stillness of my upper body as I allowed my seat to melt into his movement, and stored them away as precious memories to inspire me next time. Back in the stable yard at the end of our ride, he got his carrot and some affectionate stroking.

It is said that zazen meditation, or "just sitting," is the most perfect example of your true nature. The mind is stable, concentrated and not divided. In meditation you are the mirror reflecting the solution of your problems. This applies to riding too: It shows you (and others and the horse) your true nature. Whether sitting for zazen or on a horse, there should be no intentional, fancy way of adjusting yourself, no cheating, no pretense, and certainly no loss of focus. The attention is on the present moment, on what is, in its entirety, on being what you are. Horses, like dogs, are completely themselves; no masks, they have nothing to hide. They are who they are.

"Be like a mirror," wrote Chuang-tzu. "A mirror does not search for or create things, but welcomes and responds to all that comes before it." The world is only a mirror of ourselves, and I was finding that horseback riding held up that mirror more clearly than anything I had experienced before.

The next few weeks showed a steep curve on the learning graph. I started private lessons with Pippa on a headstrong 14-hand cob called Holly. Holly was a piebald, sturdy of body and strong of will. Holly did not tolerate fools easily. She was a good experience for me because she wanted to do what she wanted to do and I had to learn to be firm, and to insist on getting my own way with skill and not force—an appropriate life lesson in itself at this period. I learned much about technique during this time. I was riding two or three times a week, reading as much as I could between times, and using mental rehearsal.

Pippa was sweet with me. Perhaps she sensed my inner struggle as I weathered a stormy patch in my personal life, even though we never talked about it. She was down-to-earth but thoughtful, and—most important—she had a good sense of humor (that's essentially Zen, not that she was into that; she was more of a beer-down-at-the-bar-later girl). There was certainly abundant comedy available in my unskillfulness. There may be no rules in Zen, but laughter is almost mandatory: It celebrates the wit that accepts the human condition in all its magnificent silliness, and uses humor knowing it to be the deadliest of weapons against pomposity and self-righteousness. The clown is the sage; he is wisdom dressed up in a laugh.

Pippa often urged me to take things slowly, especially doing transitions from trot to canter, not to hurry, not to lurch into it.

"There's plenty of time," she said. "It's like changing gears in a car: Don't grind the gears! And look ahead, not down, just as you would when driving." I had been riding with my head down, chin dropped, watching Holly's ears as they twitched away irritably.

In slowing down from a trot to a walk, what I needed primarily was the Intention. "Remember," she explained, "horses pick up what you are thinking. All you need to do is think it. Squeezing the rein gently, relaxing into the saddle, and breathing down will be enough to halt her." She showed me

45

how to open my elbows and to curve my hands around a little in order to keep them soft.

We started to work in a 20-yard circle. The first two times we went all over the place. It was a far cry from a perfect circle. I would never have thought it would be so difficult.

"Be more assertive," Pippa called, "don't be too subtle! Look ahead to where you are going."

Then followed another of those timeless moments with which my horseback riding trajectory was punctuated, moments that remained indelibly etched on my mind. I looked ahead to the imaginary circle that we were going to ride. In doing so I must have turned my head minutely, and the rest of my body must have altered infinitesimally with the direction of the eyes. I "thought" the circle. Holly walked a perfect circle.

To me it was a miracle. The connection between my mind and my body and Holly's mind and Holly's body was so profoundly subtle, and yet so precise, that it defied belief. Yet I had experienced it. I hadn't "tried" to walk the circle, it was more like I "was" the circle. I allowed it to be, to happen, allowing the natural law of cause and effect. This essentially Zen experience exemplified that if you are trying to attain something (enlightenment for example . . . ?) you are wasting your time. The difference between those who are enlightened and those who are not, by the way, is that you don't know the difference until you realize yourself to be no better than others, in which case you are better than others. But if you think you are, you are not. Here is the paradox that rules the world. All you are doing, according to the masters, is creating and being driven by karma. If the monk (or nunk as I prefer) regards enlightenment as something to be attained, to be cultivated by discipline, he or she is guilty of the pride of self and has missed the point.

The circle I had just ridden had bypassed the ego; it was based on a perfectly merged interdependence with a fellow creature, directed through the mind. In Zen, it is the readiness of the mind that is wisdom. My life is indeed the creation of my mind.

The following week I asked Pippa what to do if a horse I was riding decided to bolt.

"Get down into the saddle and go with him," she said, "keeping a contact with the mouth. Hold the reins and guide where you can, but go with him. Don't tug the head back, otherwise, the horse will 'deaden' and won't respond to you. Don't lean forward, don't tense the shoulders, and don't panic. If you resist, tighten, scream, and panic, the horse will go faster. It'll end in disaster with your falling off and getting injured or worse."

I thought this was very funny. Riding the dragon, indeed. All the things that you would do instinctively were absolutely the wrong things. Dangerously so. So much for the primacy of the instincts. I could not imagine for one moment that if I were faced with this emergency, I would be able to relax, keep upright and balanced, not tug on the reins, and not tighten and panic. I have yet, I am happy to say, to have the experience.

We had a good lesson. She worked on relaxing my upper back, which goes tense (fear), and on relaxing my toes, which go tight (fear), and on breathing deeply to relax the abdomen, which goes tight (fear). She also worked on retaining the subtle skills of controlling from the seat and guiding with soft hands, dropping into the legs and letting them swing with the movement of the horse, and dropping into the heels: All this I had heard before, but it was painfully slow in coming together. Still, I kept nonattainment in mind, remembering that championitis does nothing for consciousness. Overreacting either way to my progress would be counterproductive: It was better not to have views on it so as neither to take pride in whatever I did "attain," nor to be discouraged because I had been too idealistic. Either of these choices would confine my practice like prison walls.

"Deepen the knees," Pippa was saying as I trotted past her, "and don't rise so high! Feel the bit: Move between her impulsion and the bit rather than up and down. Let the tummy move forward and backward." We worked until I was exhausted, and Holly stood and rested in a steam cloud of her breath while I recovered mine.

We did some work on the longe rein, which I enjoyed. The fact that Pippa was in charge of Holly meant that I could concentrate totally on my bodywork. I felt the swing of my hips with her movement in walking; I could find stillness in my upper body and hands and found a line in trotting where my shoulders came forward and feet back a little, and there was a moment when, instructed to drop into the heels, the trot felt beautiful. These moments were all too ephemeral, but somewhere somehow they must be adding up to something.

My diary reads:

Do not sit as if you are in a chair but as if standing with the legs slightly apart, with deep knees. Imagine a bubble of air between you and the saddle. Stop being so feeble with the reins—you are letting them out far too long. (I'm afraid I'll hurt the horse's mouth.)

The upper body of the rider influences the forequarters of the horse; the lower body (pelvis, legs, and hips), the hindquarters, and legs. Keep the head tall, from the waist up, shoulders open and relaxed, lifted up through the diaphragm, head balanced, neck long, tall, and proud but inwardly relaxed. Body toned and poised.

Weight forward into the center of the saddle, not back. Pelvis upright, stomach forward and upward. Stretch up from stomach and down from hips. Reins held at bit-width apart.

In trot, the hands remain the same: quiet at the base of the neck and never pulling back. The rider always projects her center of gravity toward the hands. She never brings her hands toward the body. A quiet seat, bent elbow, tender hands. The elbow is a shock absorber.

Above all, feel. *Listen to your horse, give him simple aids. The essence is purity, forwardness, clarity. Just do what comes naturally, with gravity and balance. The classical seat is the art of symmetry and balance. Keep it straightforward and simple.*

SEVEN

work without effort

Zen is not the study of Zen. Zen is life, it is direct contact with reality. Zen can only be lived and experienced. "What is the good," asked a Zen master, "of discussing a musical masterpiece? This marvelous piece must be played." Through direct experience of reality, Zen gives an illuminating insight into the true nature of things, an inner perception of reality itself without our usual masks on. This leads to the wisdom that recognizes that things are what they are, with no judgments about them. It is called "is-ness," or "suchness," in Zen.

Horseback riding is not the study of horseback riding: It can only be lived and experienced. It, too, gives illuminating insight into the nature of things, if we are awake to them. It peels off masks and demands awareness without judgment. This is the wisdom that things are simply as they are.

It was May. I had booked a hack on Rocky and drove to the stables through leafy lanes under dappled shadows that moved slightly in the breeze. The pasture outside the village was silver green in the early spring sunlight. A hare ran out of a thicket and streaked across the grass, its long ears flying out backward, bounding down the slope on strong back legs.

Karen was ready for me with Rocky, and so to my delight, was Johnny: We were to be riding out together. I patted the now-so-familiar Rocky on his burnt-brown neck, and he acknowledged me with his funny little look. As we left the road for the grass tracks, I felt the warmth of his body keeping mine warm, the swing of his hips underneath me, that movement of the quadruped that is both sideways and forward. I relaxed into the swing, feeling my hips move with it and my shoulders almost floating as my spine absorbed the graceful undulations of his walk.

Karen and Johnny went ahead chatting like old friends, and I was glad to be left quietly to enjoy the day and become absorbed in the riding. It was perfect May sunshine. Cobalt-blue bugloss and white cow parsley embroidered the green verges, buttercup meadows and cool woods lined our route. We hacked around the boundaries of the stud farm, a millionaire pad with manicured fields and immaculate fencing that ran uninterrupted for miles around. Yearlings were playing in one of the fields, racing each other up and down the meadow. It was an idyllic ride through the loveliness of England in springtime. I saw a jay flutter into one of the woods and disappear into the dense brush. I could hear the cooing of collared doves and the cheeping of hedgerow birds. On one of the canters, Johnny rode behind me, and when he caught up he came alongside.

"Your riding has really improved since I saw you in February."

"Thank you." I was pleased.

"You are so much less tense." I nodded. "It's all about being relaxed," he said.

That particular day I let my "left brain" switch off and had moments of pure "feel," with some comfortable trotting and easy canters where I felt my hips moving loosely and lightly with the horse. I was beginning to let go at last. I was full of the feeling of how much I loved doing this. I had a transcendent minute of oneness with Rocky as we trotted along the edge of a forest on a wide, grassy track. Another timeless fragment so difficult to describe, beyond words, for unskillful words can sabotage the core feeling of an experience. But it was as if he and I were one; there was only movement and energy, no self, no other, yet both and neither. It had the quality of emptiness, yet also of completeness. It was so light that there was nothing to it. Was this the paradox of experiencing nothingness?

I became aware that I was breathing into my belly, that my eyes were soft, my shoulders free, and my spine light. I was dropping into my legs just as I do in yoga, connecting with gravity and its opposite, lightness. I could now understand the paradox that any effort we make is not good for our practice because it creates waves in our minds, and the body and/or the horse picks them up. "Act without doing, work without effort. . . ." Yet the trap is, in the words of Seng-ts'an, that "when you try to stop activity to achieve passivity, your very activity fills you with activity." But if everything we do is imbued with the quality of meditation, the problem of this paradox is resolved.

You learn technique to forget technique and to subsume it in the spirit of the practice. The similarities between the two practices of riding and yoga were becoming more and more apparent. The experiences I was having on horseback were bringing more depth to my yoga practice, as well as having an impact on my everyday life. Rocky was willing and strong. I loved him and told him so as I led him back into his stable. He followed me meekly, stretching out his head alongside my shoulder, clip-clop clip-clop across the yard. His door banged behind me, and I slung the bolts across as he returned to his haynet. Hippotherapy was working on a physical level too. I had gone out with a painful sacroiliac and came home with a back that felt good.

Imagery is at the core of classical yoga. The asanas are named after animals, plants, birds, people, and gods: the cobra, the camel, the eagle, matsyendrasana, the tree, the dancer, the warrior. There are hundreds of them, symbolizing the metamorphosis that occurs when we practice, and representing our interconnectedness with the world around us, both seen and unseen. When I was teaching in this way, I could see people's bodies change infinitely subtly: "as strong as a warrior," "open the wings," "be as solid as a tree"—these words had their effect on stamina, or coordination, or balance, or alignment, or flexibility. The same applied, I discovered, to riding. Imagining the body sitting on horseback as a spruce tree had a powerful effect. With the waist at "ground" level (the saddle in this case), the spine became its slender trunk growing upward from which the branches (the shoulders) could hang down gracefully. Meanwhile the roots, the legs, "grew" strongly downward into the ground, giving stability, strength, and the ability to balance without wobbling. The head reached toward the sky, tall like the highest branches so that the upper half of the body felt light. In yoga, I tell people, more prosaically, to imagine themselves as egg timers: the legs full of sand, heavy, gravitating, the trunk empty and light. Exactly the same applies on horseback, and this image of the spruce tree, with its polarity of lightness and gravity, transformed the way I felt. The horses liked it too.

Pippa frequently dropped "right-brain" images into my lessons in order for me to move out of my accustomed "left-brain" mode (intellectual, judgmental, analytical, logical) and use my more feeling "right-brain" functions, those associated with rhythm, imagination, and spatial relationships: "Imagine you are sitting on a fluffy, white cloud. Imagine your buttocks as ice-cream scoops while you are moving in canter. Imagine, in walk, your legs are so long that they touch the ground. Imagine, in trot, that you have springs under your hips." As the weeks passed I worked with the idea of a spring pulling my abdomen forward and up to the sky, keeping centered in my abdomen and focusing the breath there. Riding with my bones, imagining myself as a skeleton, balanced me. I imagined my body full of ice cream melting and dribbling down through my feet; I pictured my forearms reaching from my elbow to the bit; I was holding the reins as if they were a pair of baby birds; and I pretended that I was a puppet hung from above by a string attached to the top of my head. To sit evenly, which was a problem for me because my left hip was tighter than my right, I imagined siphoning weight from the right leg into the left.

Pippa and I had a lot of laughs, and I enjoyed her company. She never alluded to the age difference between us, nor did she ever give signs of impatience as I struggled to find some degree of confidence and poise on horseback. I often booked lessons very early in the morning when she was still sloughing off the effects of the night before, and gradually, as she gave me snippets of autobiography, I pieced together a picture of her life with her boyfriend (her "other half" as she called him, which I found endearingly old-fashioned in one so young). We went out hacking together over that summer, sharing bits of our lives and talking horses. "Never forget," she would say, "you are the brains. The horse is the brawn."

Humphrey was certainly brawn. He was a great 17.2 Irish draft, dapple gray with long legs, wide rump, and a gigantic head that must have weighed at least 100 pounds. He was beautiful in classic working-horse style, those horses that carried armored knights into battle in medieval times. They belong to the world's biggest breed, which can reach over 6½ feet at the shoulders and weigh up to 2,500 pounds. Pippa selected him for me to hack out on with her, and I grew to love this handsome horse. It was a thrill to ride such a huge animal, steady and placid by nature but immensely strong, and feel his power under me. His long ears pricked up at the sounds around us as we rode, his nostrils alert and active. His white forelock fell lightly over his forehead between those large ears, and when he stretched out his neck to drink when we crossed a ford, I was reminded of a giraffe. He slurped the water deliciously, standing foursquare up to his ankles, and then plucked some luscious grasses from the edge of the stream, munching with obvious relish.

"Big ears mean a big heart," Pippa told me as we watched him. I stroked his neck lovingly.

The second time I rode Humphrey we walked together through the leafy lanes of Maytime into fields of green-gold barley and across an ocean of blue flax in flower. We had long trots, longer than I had ever ridden before, and this gave me the chance to get into the rhythm and feel of the movement. Humphrey seemed to enjoy it too. In our first canter, my seat was chaotic because I was tense and still frightened by his strength and speed. I could feel my shoulders and hips tightening as I bounced around in the saddle and nearly lost my stirrups as we followed Pippa up the track. He started to take off into the field, but I managed to bring him around in a circle and put the brakes on by shortening the outside rein and relaxing into the saddle. I could feel how going down into the abdomen, my center of balance, steadied both Humphrey and me. Pippa congratulated me.

"The horse wants to know that the rider is in control," she laughed. "That was good. Keep the reins short enough to give you control, and keep the hands soft, but there's all the difference in the world between that and tugging. You did well."

You are the boss, according to Zen. When the boss is sleeping, everyone sleeps; when the boss does something right, everyone does something right, and at the right time.

We rode on under a sunny sky through the blossoms and fragrances of spring: the heady scent of hawthorn, lilac in flower, a honeysuckle hedge, yellow fields of rape bordered with white cow parsley. We walked the last stretch home through the secret world of a forest where the light filtered into semigreenness, a magical theater of cheeping birds and small animals in which there are only walk-on parts for humans. Like centaurs, we passed through and out into the sunshine. Humphrey gave me a huge nuzzle when I dismounted back at the yard, nearly knocking me over. He was sweating from the heat of the sun and the vigorous ride, so I hosed him down with cold water. He stood there after I had stopped, wanting more, looking at me unfathomably with that cosmological eye that sees everything and nothing, is discriminating but not judgmental. How grateful I was for that. How few humans know how to do it—only Zen masters. I gave him his carrot and led him back to his stable.

Suspending judgment as part of the practice of Zen was being put to the test not merely in my personal life but also back at Sunnyfields Stables. Judgment defeats us; we are destroyed by holding judgments about others. Judgments are only mirrors, reflections from our own psyches, and unless we understand that, we project them onto others to our own detriment, like picking up a hot coal to throw at the enemy. This was a huge issue for me as I struggled with my relationship problems: Whatever I perceived and could so easily (because of a quick facility with words) express about the situation, how could I defer judgment on it? Even the acceptance that I fought so hard to achieve did not shift my predisposition to pronounce sentence. But take away judgment and discrimination, says Zen, and you have love. Here was my challenge.

There appeared to be a shortage of loving kindness at Sunnyfields: Madge marched around like a personification of anger, her teenage girls monosyllabic and unsmiling. Several times when I turned up for a hack that I had booked on Rocky, Madge would tell me shortly that he was unavailable and that I would have to ride another horse. Looking back (I was too inexperienced at the time to realize this), I feel she was putting my life at risk. One time she put me on Marigold, a 9-year-old chestnut, about 15 hands, whom I had noticed in the yard tossing her head from side to side over her stable door. She was sweet-natured enough, a gentle creature but nervous, especially of trucks. Five years previously she had been hit by a passing truck and been badly injured on her hindquarters and leg, and still carried the terror with her.

Nina took me out that day. She had a willowy figure, with a mass of chestnut curls framing her neat, small-featured face. She was an experienced rider who liked to do show jumping and eventing. I was not. I had the impression that she thought I belonged to a subspecies of the human race. We set off along the road and into the main highway busy with trucks and cars that didn't care at all about horses. I wished I could go home. I felt unsafe and unsupported. My heart was beating and my chest tight. I had only recently learned from my sister that horses have priority on the highway. Not many people know this, and certainly not many of those truck drivers. They thundered past us in both directions, and Marigold was petrified. She danced, she turned, she shied, she tried to take off homeward. My tactic was, in spite of my own fear, to use my voice to soothe her, and to stay in the saddle. Both worked. Nina kept turning around to yell at her not to be stupid. This had no effect. It was a nightmare. Every muscle in my body was rigid.

Somehow we arrived safely at a bridle path and left the roaring traffic behind us. I breathed again. We cantered up the path between two hedges, on one side a field of mystical blue flax, on the other young barley swept softly by a light wind. We turned off the path and onto a wide track leading up a slope.

"Okay for a gallop?" asked Nina without looking at me. It wasn't really a question.

"Um, Nina, I've only been riding for a few months and I've never galloped before. . . ."

"Oh never mind, we'll just do a fast canter then," she said, and with that she was off.

It felt like something out of the Wild West, and all those movies I had watched over a lifetime came to my rescue. Marigold charged up the hill after her—and I surrendered. I pretended to be John Wayne. For the first time I was really riding. Frightened though I was, I went with Marigold's rhythm; I relaxed into the saddle, kept my feet down into the stirrups, opened my shoulders, and let myself go with her. It was the best and longest canter so far. All my judgments and some of my fears were blown away by fully entering into the present moment and collaborating with its inevitability. I had engaged (*faute de mieux*) with what was. I felt light with relief and joy, as if the burden of opinion and criticism had been left in a heavy suitcase at the bottom of the track. I felt fully alive. Now I could understand Zen Master Dōgen's words for real, based on this experience: "Do not work for freedom, rather allow the practice itself to be liberation."

I imagined that most "good" riders couldn't possibly tell you the "how" of their riding; they just do it, they just are, with no analysis or self-consciousness. When you become you, Zen becomes Zen. No effort. When you are you, you see things as they are, and you become one with your horse and with your surroundings. Being yourself, without fear, this is the lesson of riding just as it is of Zen. "Become the one you are" was Goethe's favorite maxim.

A covey of partridges flew up from under the hedge, calling raucously, and as I got my breath back I watched them fly low over the field, wings chirring. Marigold stood quietly. Patting her neck, I thanked her for the nearest experience to flying that I had ever had, for being my Pegasus for 5 minutes. Then we continued our ride and our dances with trucks.

EIGHT

present moment

At the end of May, I had my first ride on Jade down at Rushbrook. This fine 16.2 hunter-mare belonged to Helen's husband. Since he worked in London all week and could only ride her on weekends, she needed as much exercise as she could get. I was one of the lucky riders. A rich brown with shades of chestnut, she had a touch of working horse in her. She was strong and well proportioned with a beautiful head, her mane cropped short and stiff as a thick brush, giving her a punk look. For all her vigor and strength she was, Pippa assured me, very easygoing.

Several riders were busy with their horses in the yard as we crossed to the mounting block. A huge horse box was being loaded up, the horses clattering up the ramp into their compartments. Pippa drew back her long, fair hair and tied it into a knot on the top of her head.

"That's better. It's so hot today." She was wearing a skimpy T-shirt and leggings, and heavy walking boots. She led Jade into the new dressage ring, which had just been completed. It was 60 feet long and solidly fenced, lined by mature trees on one side and the indoor school on the other. A bank of elders in full flower gave out its grapey scent in the sunshine; a briar rose clambered high into the hedge behind it. Tiny white stars of stitchwort peeped above the long grass behind the sturdy fencing. From the top of the school, I could see the low-lying paddocks running down to the river where some of Helen's other horses were grazing contentedly. I was aware of the sound of Jade's hooves swishing through the fine slate-gray gravel, the rhythmical swing of her proud walk, the sun on my face.

"Let your hands move with her mouth in walk, but keep them still while trotting. Keep that elastic feel with the mouth. Think of your hands guiding her as if you were riding a bike. Keep 'talking' to her with your hands—if you keep a 'conversation' going with her mouth, she will know where to go and what to do. Don't, on the other hand, become too 'busy' with the hands, particularly when you change gait. But if you lose contact, she will feel lonely."

We worked on my seat, on dropping more into the heels, keeping the feet loose and relaxed. "Nudge her with a 'tap-tap' of your legs to move her on," said Pippa as she followed me around. I rode without stirrups, crossing them over the front of the saddle and feeling my legs lengthen, my hips loosen and open. But my toes still tightened instinctively when I started a new gait. The familiar instruction to keep the hips relaxed and the legs wide still did not deter me from gripping with the knees when we went into a canter. My fear had deep roots.

"Keep your hands light and in contact with the horse's head as it moves up and down," called Pippa as I raced past her. "Keep your head up: You still have a tendency to drop your chin and look down. Don't duck!" We slowed down into a trot and then came to a halt. I patted Jade's neck and she turned her head to look at me impassively. She was beautiful.

"What position do I get into if I want to gallop?" I asked Pippa.

She giggled. "I don't think she's going to bolt inside the school."

"But if I'm out on a hack and Dulcie gets the bit between her teeth, so to speak, and takes off with me, given that I have to ride her and if I can't stop her, I need to know how to do it."

"Point taken," said Pippa. "Let's go into the back paddock and I'll show you."

We walked out of the ring and across the yard to a five-bar gate. Pippa opened it for us and we went through into a small field. She told me to halt Jade and stand quietly.

"You get your heels down and take your seat out of the saddle like this." She reached up and guided my body into position. "Then lean forward toward the neck, keeping the reins short. You can hold on to the mane if you like."

So for the first time in my life I went into a gallop around the field, clutching Jade's thick brush of a mane. I had to stay totally focused both on every part of her movement and on my own position. The concentration was intense, and probably an intrinsic part of the enjoyment. The mindfulness that arises from this degree of concentration is single-pointed; the mind is not divided between one thing or another. I had to be there in the present moment: Any thought, whether of fear or judgment or self-consciousness, would have unbalanced both of us.

When you sit in zazen meditation, you are wholly present, single-pointed, with no judgments and no ambition to "become." You just are. Then as your practice deepens, you understand that whatever you do is zazen. "Ordinary" things are given the same mindful attention as zazen. In a sense, this gallop was meditation in action, it was zazen, yet I was only doing something that mankind has done every day for millennia, but because it was new to me I was—like a child learning a new skill—totally there. Zen is not a special or separate activity; it is concentration on ordinary, everyday things. It is an experience, not a bundle of dogma and words. The idea is to live from moment to moment, being yourself. There was no way, as a beginner, that I could maintain this gallop on Jade in any other way. Zen is awakening to whatever we are doing, because most of the time we do things automatically, as if we are not there. "When sitting, just sit. When walking, just walk. Above all, don't wobble." The classic satori (or enlightenment) experience of carrying wood or drawing water is absorption in an everyday activity that induces wonder at the mystery of life: There is no enlightenment outside of ordinary life, no "buddhahood" besides the everyday mind.

So seldom are we present in the present moment. We are nowhere (the word "nowhere" is made up of "now" and "here," an apt reminder to correct ourselves). We drag the past around with us, we dream of the future. There was no place for any of that as Jade and I flew around the paddock. I had to be completely awake. "In the heart of this moment is eternity," wrote the 13th-century monk Meister Eckhart. Horseback riding was verifying this mystic experience for me. Riding seemed to be the ultimate in mindfulness, in absorption, in being present, being there. Those timeless moments experienced within time remain engraved in my memory with an intense clarity, and still inspire awe at both their beauty and their ordinariness. Each one was about being totally present, totally alive. And then it was gone.

Breathless, I slowed into a canter and then down into a steady trot. Jade was panting as I patted her neck, damp with perspiration.

"Well done," grinned Pippa. "Not bad at all. That's all for today. Would you like to put Jade back in her stable?"

This beautiful golden horse walked me back through the yard swinging her hips, her head relaxed and neck long. I swung down off her, feeling happy and elated, and took off her saddle. She gave me an affectionate nuzzle before I led her into her stable. I had fallen in love—again.

The next lesson was a revelation. Pippa got me to ride with my eyes closed. She wanted me to "feel" instead of thinking too much and trying to work it all out in my head. In walking I could feel as never before the sideways movement from the quarters as well as the forward impulsion with its wavelike rhythm.

"Think of giving your boots a shine on her sides," called Pippa. "Move your tummy toward the hands, keeping down in the saddle but with the feeling of someone pulling you up to the sky by a single hair. Light and loose. Light and loose."

It was brilliant. When riding with my eyes open, thinking had been taking me away from what was really happening—it captured me inside my head. Closing my eyes, I could "think unthinkingly." Feeling her walking with that elegant, rhythmical swing, there was only the present moment. Even more so in trotting: I relaxed my hips, opened my knees as I came lightly down into the saddle, and allowed my hips to move with her. Keeping the feet stationary remained a problem, but I didn't feel the need to control so much as I had in the thinking, eyes-wide-open mode. Doing it with "feel," my mind did not get in the way. So, I rejoiced, all this thinking gets in the way! Without it, I could "just be" with Jade. As Seng-ts'an put it:

> *The more you talk and think about it, the further astray you wander from the truth.*
> *Stop talking and thinking, and there is nothing you will not be able to know.*

Cantering with my eyes closed was even better. We went around in a 20-yard circle, and I could feel it the moment that she went off the line. As she began to fall out of the circle, I brought her back with my legs. This was a triumph, a big moment, feeling it rather than thinking it. My ice-cream scoops came into their own as I moved easily with her rocking-horse canter. I felt my shoulders relax and my spine lengthen. Now was the time, I decided, to let go and *feel* my riding.

The next time I rode Dulcie, we went into her easy, rocking-horse canter and I felt the control from the seat, the guiding with the hands that went with the movement of her head, my shoulders relaxed and my seat soft and easy. I felt light and loose in the trot and controlled her speed from my seat by rising either faster or more slowly. It was over all too soon. It always was: These times on horseback seldom felt long enough. Today it all seemed so easy.

> *Easy is right. Begin right*
> *And you are easy.*
> *Continue easy and you are right.*
> *The right way to go easy*
> *Is to forget the right way*
> *And forget that the going is easy.*
> —Chuang-tzu

NINE

"above all, don't wobble"

Y ou'd better watch out; I think I might steal Jade. If she goes missing, you'll know where to look," I told Pippa when I arrived for my next lesson. What a perfect horse she was.

Pippa smiled. "And you're not the only one who feels that way," she said. "She's lovely."

We walked around the school to warm her up, and I felt lucky to have found such a beautiful mare to share this new challenge in my life, which had brought me many unexpected pleasures and had so much to teach me. I relaxed into her rolling walk, talking softly to her and feeling the contact with her mouth on the reins. Her ears were busy picking up my signals and also taking in what was going on outside the ring in the yard. Putting my hand on her withers, I watched her glossy, powerful shoulders move under me. *O le bel aujourd-hui.*

It was indeed a lovely day. Birds were chattering their dialogue from the tall hedgerow that ran alongside the school, under a gentle sky that threw soft shadows over the gravel. The fine weather had lingered for 3 weeks, unusually, and it had not rained for a month. Things came together and I was able to let go, to relax, to feel light and loose. The minute I stopped "trying" and stopped thinking, everything fell into place. Then there were moments of oneness, of lightness, almost of invisibility, as if nothing was happening and as if I wasn't there. Zen masters say that when you do something you should burn yourself completely like a good fire, leaving no vestige of yourself, like the eagle who leaves no trace when it flies. These fleeting moments came and went like flames that flicker and disappear into nothingness. They could not be grasped, for like any experience of joy, they cannot be bound. After all, said Nietzsche, "Man is not made for happiness, but for moments of happiness."

"I think you're ready to try some dressage movements," said Pippa. "Think of it as 'yoga for horses'! We'll start with leg yielding. Remember, you are guiding with your hands and controlling with your seat and legs."

We started to walk down the school on the three-quarter

line; two-thirds of the way down I had to walk her sideways to the fence. It worked perfectly.

"Must have been beginner's luck," I said to Pippa as we prepared to do it a second time. I was right. It didn't always work so easily. But then, that first time, I wasn't letting anticipation or thinking get in the way.

Walking a straight line on a horse is not as simple as it might sound. But it appeared that if I looked ahead at where I wanted to go, without wavering, completely focused, Jade would also go without wavering so long as I kept hands and legs balanced. This seemed miraculous to me. But the Zen masters would not have been astonished. "When walking, just walk. Don't wobble. . . ." The sideways walk, leg yielding, to the fence seemed quite easy, turning my head to look to the opposite corner which turned my shoulders slightly to balance her. We tried it in a trot, too, and after several attempts began to make a smooth, curved line in the fine gravel of the dressage ring.

"Relax your toes!" called Pippa. "You can even turn your feet out a little in order to release your hips. Don't *try* too hard! Simplification, that's what you need. Simplify, simplify!"

The lesson ended with a long canter around the school for Jade to let off steam and for me to practice keeping my heels down and getting to relax into the saddle as if I was on a rocking horse instead of being bounced out of the saddle (which was still happening). We walked together out of the school.

"I'm going on vacation in a couple of weeks," Pippa said, "so if you'd like you could ride Jade on your own in the school and practice some of what we did today."

I was thrilled. It seemed such a grown-up thing to do. This is what I had been wishing: I thought it apt that I had just seen how, on horseback, if you look ahead in the direction you want to go, you get there. As in life, I mused, look ahead at your goal, don't wobble, and it will happen. Your life is the creation of your mind. . . . But I felt scared, too: I had never yet tacked up a horse on my own, so Pippa said that next time I could tack up Jade myself and she would supervise me. Over the next couple of sessions I fumbled my way around bridles and girths and bits and curb-chains (feeling ham-fisted and clumsy), and this was difficult for me. I felt deeply uncomfortable, like an inadequate child, as Pippa watched my stupid mistakes. Emotionally fragile as I was, I was often close to tears and had to swallow hard to keep them back. Humphrey's bridle had a martingale and seemed as complicated as crochet. I was all thumbs. The many humbling, not to say humiliating, experiences of the steep learning curve that I was climbing, of everything to do with horses and riding, were, however, compensated by the nonjudgmental acceptance of my Zen masters, the horses: Jade, Humphrey, and Dulcie all stood patiently each time, responding to my voice and my hands as I prepared them—so incompetently—to go out.

My diary recorded the following two lessons in some detail: We were in the indoor school for the first one, practicing 20-yard circles, then going down from 20 to 10, keeping an eye on a cone at the center of the circle. This was done with leg yielding, guiding with the hands—and above all "thinking" the circle and never taking my eye off the cone. The nanosecond my concentration lapsed, we wavered, and the true line fell apart. "When riding, just ride. Don't wobble. . . ." Thinking about being attached by a piece of elastic to the cone as if it drew me inward helped keep the spiral line even. I was repeatedly amazed at how Jade picked up what was in my mind. My childhood fascination for geometry, to some extent satisfied by the invisible human geometry of yoga, was being rekindled by riding.

A circle is a continuum. It starts nowhere and ends nowhere. I had to learn how not to "begin" and "end" the circle but to accept it as this continuum (very Zen, no beginning, no end. Don't "do" the circle, "be" the circle). In yoga, in balancing postures, the body adjusts to the eyes (just try standing on one leg and then shutting your eyes and you will understand how we use our eyes to balance us). Likewise on horseback: If you look

ahead and fractionally inward at your circle, the body balances
with infinitesimal subtlety, and the horse picks it up. As we
worked on the circle, Pippa taught me how the coordination
between outside leg (nudging—with calves and ankles, not
feet) and inside rein needs to be gentle but also positive so that
the horse knows who is boss. We did this while trotting, too,
for a long time, until I was sweating and exhausted. If this was
doing nothing else for me, it was getting me fit!

I did some long canters on 20-yard circles, gradually learning
to control the pace with my seat (down, relaxed) and the outside rein (squeeze rather than yank). I practiced changing di-
agonals in a trot. When the outside shoulder goes back is when
I am down in the saddle. I began to feel easy and light in the
stride—and this improved immeasurably once I looked up and
used the "soft eyes" of peripheral vision. I felt it all coming together, and Pippa was pleased with me, both in trotting and in
cantering. Then I made my first attempt at transitions from a
trot to a canter, and from a canter down to a trot, which felt like
fun (even though I was inept). We did more leg yielding and
20- to 10-yard spirals. I resolved to try all this the following session on my own with Jade when Pippa was on vacation.

The following Thursday, I drove to the stables during lunch
hour with fear in my gut. The butterflies in my stomach got

worse as I turned onto the road that led to the yard. I wished I hadn't gotten myself into this. It felt like taking a major exam: I wished I wasn't there. *Why* was I doing this to myself, I asked.

Nobody was around. The stable hands were all having lunch, and the school was empty. Nervously I walked over to Jade's stable and greeted her with a carrot and a pat on the neck. I went into the tack room and lifted the heavy saddle off its rack with its girth attached, and walked through to put it over the stable door. Then I returned to pick up the bridle. My hat and stick were lying on the concrete outside the stable door, so I put on my hat and stuck my stick down into my boot. I felt disorganized; where should I put the bridle while I saddled her? I felt panicky. There was obviously a system for doing things in the right order and putting things in the right place; otherwise you could get seriously confused, but I hadn't worked it out. My feelings of inadequacy were becoming familiar: the sinking heart, the uncomfortable stomach, the tight feeling in the shoulders. I wished I were somewhere else.

I went into the stable and closed the door behind me. I inhaled the musk of clean straw, Jade's sweet horse smell, the leather of the saddle. Her hooves made a lazy clop as she moved toward the wall to nibble at her hay, her long, loose tail falling almost to the ground. As I stepped toward her, she made a sudden movement that made my heart leap into my mouth. How powerful she was at such close quarters. I was frankly terrified.

I knew I had to tack her up from the left side, but Jade had decided to stand with her left side firmly against the wall. I wished Pippa were there with all my heart. Taking a deep breath, I decided that my voice was probably my most useful tool, so I tried persuasion, cajoling her softly. She just looked at me. It was clear that I was going nowhere with that tactic. Okay, I thought, who is boss? So I raised my voice and told her to cooperate, got myself between the wall and her magnificent flank, leaned against her, and pushed against her considerable weight. She moved.

Saddling her was simple enough. The bridle took longer as I fumbled my way through its intricacies. It was with some sense of triumph mixed with relief that I led her out of the stable and through the yard to the mounting block. Once mounted, I tightened the girth from above, awkwardly, aware that the girls could see me from the office where they were eating their sandwiches. I tried not to care.

Luckily the gate to the dressage school was open. I realized that if it hadn't been, I would have had to dismount, open it, lead Jade back to the mounting block, and start all over again, no doubt much to the amusement of the unseen spectators. Next time I would check that it was open before I mounted. I leaned to close it behind me but couldn't reach. How do people do that, I wondered? (I asked someone later and they said that someone has to do it for you. I hadn't been as useless as I had thought.) So we spent our session there with the gate open, which was not ideal since on several occasions as we rode toward it, Jade thought it was an invitation to return to her stable. Horses are "homers" and have a gravitational pull toward the security of their patch, where food and comfort are provided.

We had half an hour in the dressage school practicing 20- to 10-yard circles, leg yielding, and transitions, not very successfully. Gradually I relaxed into absorption as the tensions of what had seemed like an ordeal dissolved. I felt the joy of riding as we worked, a growing exhilaration at the freedom of some degree of independence. Untacking her was no problem: I stabled her with the gift of a final carrot and a sense of a major obstacle overcome, with huge relief at Mission Accomplished. It began to rain as I walked back to the car under the trees. I stood and listened to it pattering and rustling on the leaves and watched a bee forage deep into a thistle flower. The long drought was over.

TEN

no becoming,
just being

As the month of June passed into July, I hacked out from Sunnyfields with Karen or Nina on various horses. One day I was lucky enough to get Rocky again, and we had a relaxed ride. I felt my seat deep in the saddle, my body light during long trots where I concentrated on keeping my hands and feet still, my shoulders open but soft, and the feeling loose but strong.

There was a memorable ride on a new horse called Rosie, a 12-year-old dark bay mare, 15.2 hands with a skinny, uncoordinated body and a sprightly personality. Nina took me on a fast hour-and-a-half circuit made up almost entirely of trotting and cantering along grassy tracks. I had the feeling that she was testing me. A haze of speedwell rose from the lane that led out to the fields; midsummer grasses turned into a drift of silver as they caught the light. The wheat was ripening into fields of gold, and the ground was soft after a week of rain. Today, though, the sun shone and the day was beautiful as we cantered past the blue-green barley on one side, catching a streak of scarlet poppies in the wheatfield on the other side. Baby partridges risked their lives as they scampered across the track under our thundering hooves into the cover of the crops. Although Rosie had an easy rhythmical trot and the movement felt effortless, her canter was a different matter. She moved like a crab, sideways, and this gave me a great opportunity to practice staying in the saddle. I realized that I wasn't having to think about how I was sitting or what I should do: It was feeling connected. I was feeling rather than thinking, using my "right brain" rather than my "left brain."

We had long trots and uninterrupted canters through this paradise of a landscape, ducking under low branches as we passed through forest and emerged into meadows where lambs were playing around their ewes. The only thing that matters, I mused, is now—and God, how it matters. I was here, now, yet nowhere, in the pure pleasure of being, with no thought of becoming. No ambition; it was enough—and more—to be in this present moment. I felt at one with my destiny and reconciled to whatever it might throw at me, without fear, because this sense of the blessing of the present was so strong. On our return to the stables, Rosie gave me a huge nuzzle before I offered her her well-deserved carrot.

The next ride with Sunnyfields was a complete contrast. I took my niece, Kirsty, along for a treat, hoping perhaps to repeat this same circuit. The day was wet and cold, the ground soft and squelchy after days of incessant rain. Nina didn't say a word to either of us as we mounted. I asked if we could go the same route as last week, but she did not reply. We did a dreary round along roads and short tracks, the horses slipping and sliding in the slithering mud. At one point the rain came down in sheets and soaked us to the skin, turning us blue with cold. I was grateful for the steamy warmth of Rosie's body. Throughout the hour, Nina never spoke to us. We were walking single file downhill along a narrow lane to an intersection, the horses slipping occasionally on the wet tarmac. A young boy in a car came hurtling off the main road into the lane, and skidded across the center line, only narrowly missing us. "A******," she yelled at him, then turned her back on us and led on to cross the main road. When we dismounted in the stable yard, she walked away without a word. I decided I could no longer deal with her offhandedness. My skin was not thick enough. I resolved never to ride there again. How sad I was to forgo riding through such exceptionally beautiful countryside, but I couldn't handle these people who refused to have a civilized relationship with their clients and who gave me horses that were unsuitable and sometimes dangerous for me to ride. We returned home soaked, miserable in body and spirits. I felt choked with a mixture of sadness and anger, my heart was heavy at the thought of Rocky who had become such a good, solid friend, of never seeing him again. He had given me so much. It was a parting of ways, and the feeling of loss, not unmixed with anger, lasted for a long while afterward.

Once back in my cottage, Kirsty and I warmed up with mugs of spicy soup and some bread and agreed to go out the following week on Dulcie and Tandy, and to put the experience behind us. It had been a bad day.

The afternoon was limpid, one of those July days when nature looks tired, when even the birds can't be bothered to sing and a few desultory insects hang around. Even though the past week had seen some rainfall, the ground had dried out quickly and was cracking open in parts where the heavy clay had hardened. The trees had grown out of their spring cloaks of many greens and wore the uniform dark green foliage of high summer. We groomed the horses together, scraping dried mud off their strong coats with steel combs, working carefully around the eye area. Dulcie had evidently found a wet patch somewhere down by the pond in a low-lying part of the paddock and had had a good roll in it. Duly cleaned and tacked up, we walked the horses out into the lanes, meandering through a small wood where Dulcie stopped to relieve herself. As she arched her tail, she came to a stop, handbrake fully engaged. The droppings fell to the ground in soft thuds, sweet-smelling piles of manure behind her heavy feet. I felt her breathing. She turned her head to view the evidence, looked pleased with herself, gave a little blow through her nostrils, and moved on placidly, making a dignified exit from the scene of the crime.

Kirsty and I chatted as we rode on, and she asked me whether I was going to learn to jump.

"Absolutely not," I said. "I decided right at the beginning that it is far too dangerous. Look at what happened to Christopher Reeve. I am too old for those tricks, and I just don't want to take unnecessary risks. Horseback riding is dangerous enough as it is. They say it rates higher on the danger scale than formula-one racing."

"Oh, you ought to try it sometime. Jumping's easy, really."

"Kirsty," I reminded her in auntlike fashion, "don't forget, you've been riding for, what—8 years?"

She nodded.

"So it's all right for you to talk! If I had started as a child, like you did, I would have loved to learn to jump. But not at my age."

She laughed. "Don't be silly. You're not old. It's so much fun!"

"No, really, I made up my mind about it early on. And anyway, I get so much pleasure from hacking out, and the work in the schooling ring. That's more than enough for me."

We trotted and cantered around the edge of a farm on wide, grassy tracks feeling relaxed and carefree, especially in Dulcie's rocking-horse canter. She was racing with Tandy as we flew like the wind along a wide path that ran beside a high hedgerow, iron shoes ringing on the hard ground. I had a blurred glimpse of bramble in flower and cream clusters of hogweed. The track started to curve around to the right.

"I'd better warn you," Kirsty called to me, "there's a log across the end of this path just around the corner. Dulcie sometimes jumps it. You could always have a go—it's only a log."

"Okay," I said.

To this day, I don't know why I said it. I had just stated quite clearly my decision not to jump. But I felt confident and safe on the now familiar Dulcie. I was not prepared for the jump, partly because we were going so fast and partly because I didn't know how to prepare for the movement anyway. I was thrown off to the left, and all I remember is a massive blow to my head. For a split second, everything went black, then I saw stars and realized that Dulcie was standing a few yards away from me. The ground under my back was rock hard. I rolled sideways to get up, feeling so stunned that I had to kneel for a while to recover as Kirsty dismounted and ran to catch Dulcie's reins. (She wasn't going anywhere—she had found a patch of lush grass, and the needs of the stomach are paramount in Dulcie's world.)

"Are you all right?" Kirsty asked, evidently shaken and worried.

"I think so. I'll be okay in a minute."

I took my time to get up; nothing seemed amiss.

"You fell in the right way," said Kirsty. "You curled up, and that's what you're supposed to do. But I'm really sorry. I should have made us slow down and walk around the log. Are you sure you're okay?"

"Don't worry," I reassured her, "it was my own fault. I was stupid and made a silly decision when I was unprepared. It's taught me a lesson."

I was aware that I was somewhat characteristically not allowing myself to acknowledge what had happened, partly to protect Kirsty and to make her feel all right about it, partly to deny to myself what could have happened. I climbed back into the saddle, and as we rode homeward I reassured Kirsty that she must not take the blame. I felt fine, I said. We trotted and even cantered a little to get my confidence back. When we had put the horses back into the paddock, I climbed into my car.

"Are you really sure you're okay to drive?"

"Yes, honestly, I'm fine."

As I drove home, I realized that I needed that fall to teach me something. I had been feeling confident and comfortable, which was all very well, but I had forgotten how vulnerable I was on horseback. I had been irresponsible. Above all, it was a lesson in mindfulness: The minute you are not focused, you run enormous risks because things happen with split-second timing in riding and horses react without warning, whether to a bird making a sudden movement, or to an insect bite, or to an unexpected noise. You have to be prepared for anything, at any time. The body follows the mind, and if the mind is not clear the body gets muddled. I had been mentally unprepared. (How much of my life did I spend like that?)

It was when I got home and went to get out of the car that I realized that I was far from "okay." My lower back had seized up, and I could barely walk indoors. It was then that the full impact of the fall began to emerge. Suddenly I felt very fragile and frightened. I hardly dared to think how much worse it could have been. I spent the rest of the evening moving around tentatively and doing gentle stretches specifically designed for lower-back pain. I took arnica (a homeopathic remedy), had a hot bath before bed to relax my body, and imagined it would all be better in the morning. I was wrong.

It was considerably worse. I had experienced the magic effects of endorphins on the body. Instantaneously released into the body on impact, their anesthetic effect had allowed me to remount, ride home, even trot and canter, and then drive. The following day, and for many days afterward, I could have done none of those things. Everyday life had to be canceled for over a week while my body dealt with the effects of falling heavily on concrete-hard ground onto my tailbone, impacting the sacrum. This area of my back had been unstable for a while in the first place; it was a weak spot, and I had damaged it severely. I spent the days fluctuating between pain and fear. My body ached, my head felt strangely light, and I could move only with care. I was not sure that I ever wanted to ride again. In one carefree moment, in the casting of caution to the wind, the experience of riding had taken on the dimension of nightmare.

ELEVEN

life lessons

What had happened was that I had fallen heavily onto my back, landing on my tailbone, and then received a blow to the head from a flying hoof. Fortunately (to say the least), my riding hat was state-of-the-art and had protected my skull from terrible injury. As the days went by, I realized what a lucky escape I had had. The hoof could have landed in my face, or if the hat had not been so good . . . A deep level of shock came out during the days that followed, a realization of the nearness of death or disfigurement. It gave me a sense of how my brain is my most precious asset and, however obvious that might be, it was a pivotal truth that took on a new meaning for me. Brain is beautiful. Your life is the creation of your mind. . . .

The period of recovery after the accident gave me the impetus to look at my life and to reassess priorities. What had I done so far with my life, and what did I regret not having done? It was a valuable time. I covered the pages of my journal with lists and dreams. From my cottage sanctuary, I could hear the bustle of harvest. Combines crawled past the window along the village street and out into the fields behind my garden. Like lumbering dinosaurs, they devoured the crops, rumbling and roaring through the ghosts of working horses that had plodded over past harvest fields under the plow. Grain trailers rushed from field to field, clattering down the street from field to barn, barn to field again, collecting the harvested grain for storage.

For the first few days, I was in severe pain and afraid that I might have injured my coccyx permanently; that I would never ride again; that my yoga would be limited by a chronically impaired flexibility. Had I thrown away my precious mobility, fitness, and suppleness? As it became clear that at worst I had only bruised some bones, I felt intense relief and gratitude and began to make specific resolutions. I outlined new goals for myself. If the fall turned out to be a life lesson in itself, it also made me look at other life lessons that riding had taught me over the past 10 months.

I sat in the garden at twilight watching huge shadows of the combine dance on the trees as it gobbled and throbbed its way through the wheat. It staggered past the hedge like a giant with huge eyes of light, silhouetting my sycamore against the August night. I looked up into the stars in the darkening sky. Cassiopeia looked down unmoved. Dew rose under my insignificant bare feet.

Humility was the big one. Starting at zero on a learning curve and being like a helpless child had had its fair share of humiliations: These had taught me to receive the experience with a humble mind rather than with defensive judgments or in the spirit of attrition. Secondly, I had been made to wake up, because both mindfulness and heightened awareness are of paramount importance in the presence of horses. ("Be wide awake, Ānanda," said the Buddha to his disciple.) Thirdly, tenacity had been essential. Many had been the moments of despair when I had wanted to give up, and it had taken an effort of will to stay the course. Honesty, self-control, patience, and sensitivity were all essential qualities, it seemed to me, in good horseback riding. Equanimity and generosity are needed more in riding than in any other sport, because success does not depend solely on human effort. I had learned some of the extraordinarily subtle communication skills possible between horse and rider, and a realization of the need for integrity in dealing with horses, the necessity of accepting them as they are while at the same time being truly myself: the mirror of truth held up one to another. I pondered this as I floated into sleep. The next morning, the smell of cut straw drifted into the garden in a haze of harvest dust. The last of the old-fashioned roses drooped their heads.

Riding had taught me about the art of not trying; about letting go; about being present; about the subtle reality of cause and effect; about relationship and how everything we encounter is relationship and how much I enjoy that. I learned to control by going with and understanding the horses; to be more assertive, realizing that I could be stronger than I thought, without hurting them; about how age is nothing, it is immaterial, and that everything is about attitude—it is all in the thinking; about how oversensitive I can be, to the point of paranoia, and that for my own self-protection I could be tougher; and about the pure joy of riding in the countryside in harmony with a beautiful and powerful animal, practicing skill in action.

I had gained in self-confidence, in the sense of making an unthought-of exploration and pushing myself through thresholds I would never have dreamed of before. I was facing my fears every time I rode. I was setting goals, even if little ones, to improve my skills. I was tuning in to how to relax while concentrating, and to my limited capacity for problem-solving, as well as to the need for mental flexibility. My physical coordination and balance were being put to the test constantly, as was my personal accountability. I experienced with horses the need for compassion with authority. The teamwork implicit in horsemanship was a life lesson for someone who spends so much time alone and who revels in solitude. Above all, the contact with horses had brought a certain solace to my soul.

It was like a bereavement, being unwell over harvest time. To my slight horror I took up watching horse racing on television, but really I longed to be out there walking the lanes and riding through the stubble, smelling freshly cut wheat under the sweltering sky of late summer. I was missing the spectacle of harvest even though I could hear it and smell it. Every time a combine rolled its noisy way through the village, I was reminded of my incapacity. In the evening, I watched from my window as an orange sun sank behind the shorn fields, silhouetting bales of neatly rolled straw that sat on the stubble in the harvest sunset.

It was nearly 3 weeks before I could ride again. I was unsure of how I would feel back in the saddle, so I booked an early morning hack with Pippa, on Humphrey. I caressed his dappled neck as he towered above me, glad to breathe in his sweet horse smell. I realized how much I had missed the smell of leather and the musk of the horses. He felt like an old friend.

Placid and steady though he was, I felt myself back at the beginning again with my fear: I was rigid and awkward to start with, finding it impossible to connect back to the relaxed awareness with which I had just begun to ride. Until my mind settled into the rhythms of the riding, my body was stiff and unyielding, my toes stiffening in a primitive fear response every time we picked up speed. However, a gentle hour under a scudding sky did much to steady my confidence. The barley was ready for harvest, mellow gold between the dark trees. I noticed a cobweb spun like a hammock over some long grasses, glistening with dew.

I need not have worried: Within 2 weeks I was back to where I had left off, and a long hour-and-a-half hack one Sunday morning on Humphrey revived the feeling of pure happiness as we cantered light and loose in the sunshine, inhaling the heavy scent of yarrow as Humphrey's hooves crushed wild grasses along the track. I felt easy, comfortable, and confident again, and when I arrived at a friend's house afterward she said she had never seen me looking so radiant—hot, sweaty, and smelly though I was. "Yes," I wrote in my diary that day, "I love it. This wonderful discovery is the most joyful and pleasurable thing in my life." So much had happened since my first tentative peek behind the looking glass that day at harvest time nearly a year before.

TWELVE

surrender,
and trust

It wasn't until the end of August that I rode Jade again. She engaged in a long nuzzle as I talked softly to her in her stable. I stroked her nose and looked into her big brown eye. Jade of the sable-soft coat was forward-going that day, eager to move for me, so much so that as we started walking around the school, I wondered where my safety belt was (undoubtedly a residue of the accident and a feeling that recurred occasionally when I hadn't ridden for a while). I felt high up and exposed for several minutes before readjusting my mind and relaxing down into the saddle.

During the last weeks of harvest, I spent a lot of time in the school with Jade on our own, practicing simple dressage movements over and over in order to feel them rather than do them. Thinking them yet not thinking them, and trying to disconnect from goal orientation. My circles became more fluent (sometimes), the leg yielding more coordinated (leg yielding is when the horse moves away from the rider's inside leg, crossing his legs in front to move diagonally). This exercise began to happen more from the seat and less from the forehand. Being on the forehand means that the horse is using his shoulders more than his quarter and that the rider moves with the front of his body. I began to relax into my transitions, seeing them as a change of gait rather than a change of speed, so instead of contemplating acceleration, I would think "canter," not "faster." When slowing down, I began to breathe down into the saddle with a half halt on the outside rein, as a movement on the bit rather than on the head or neck, which worked only when I kept my mind fully focused. I used the image of dropping a heavy chain down through both our centers deep into the ground to anchor us: It stopped us beautifully—usually. I still got upset with myself when it went badly or the images didn't work or I bounced around in the saddle out of sync with Jade. I like to excel. This is not helpful, as I was learning from my Zen masters, both human and equine.

The principal instruction to the British Olympic dressage team from their German trainer is, "Let go." You let go, you let the horse go, allowing him to extend, and then you can collect him. It is done by how you sit and how you breathe. Henry Miller had much to say on this score: "When you surrender," he wrote in *Big Sur*, "the problem ceases to exist. Try to solve it, to conquer it, and you only set up more resistance. You alone control nothing." He pointed out that life only begins when you give up the struggle and drop beneath the surface, to a deeper understanding, and that true strength lies in submission. "It's when you renounce, when you surrender, that miracles happen. Instead of surrendering to life, we struggle to avoid dying." To live dangerously means putting trust in the life force instead of battling with the phantoms of fear. The key word is trust; it is a prerequisite. Trust everything that happens in life, even—and especially—those experiences that cause pain. Without an underlying trust that all will be well, you are paralyzed by the past. Zen is based in that natural trust that children have, whose fruits are spontaneity and understanding. Suspicion, like its close relative fear, is a strangler.

The rider is an artist, a sculptor; the horse the medium in which he or she works. That Olympic trainer knew that you don't have to be a big person physically, but powerful mentally. The 19th-century German philosopher Hegel's maxim that "thought ought to govern spiritual reality" acknowledges the primacy of the mind. The paradox is that the strong, focused mind also knows the wisdom of surrender. Mental surrender brings calmness in the wake of trust, and also acceptance. Acceptance was a big word for Henry Miller:

> *Accepting life as it is, seeing what it is and taking it for what it is, not having illusions and delusions about it . . . When we speak of a person accepting himself for what he is, we do not simply mean that he admits and recognizes his weaknesses but that he also discovers how important they were in his evolution. . . . Acceptance is the key word. But acceptance is precisely the stumbling block. It has to be total acceptance and not conformity. Nothing can arrest the pain of birth unless it is the acceptance of the miraculous nature of one's own being. Everything that happens is a doorway to liberation.*
> —Reflections

Animals have much to teach about acceptance. Once trust is established, they are capable of manifesting a total acceptance of humankind in unquestioning surrender. They seem to trust the basic rhythm of life in a way that humans do not. It is axiomatic in Zen not to struggle, but to go with the flow of things in order to find yourself at one with the unity of the universe. Surrender is a central quality of Zen, letting go of concepts, of self, of conditioning, in order to move into the purity and simplicity of what is. Do not struggle.

I wrote in my diary after one particularly rewarding session with Jade:

Surrendering means allowing, not forcing, not trying. It means undoing, not doing, dropping down yet extending up (just as in yoga). What riding is teaching me is trust. Trust above all, based on understanding. I never trusted horses until I began to understand them a little. Now, with more skills, I can trust implicitly and make progress. I am doing this through relationships other than human ones. And why not? The Buddha says that it is better to travel alone than to travel in the companionship of a fool.

That morning, when I opened the front door of the cottage, I stepped into a new landscape of open fields shaven to stubble that scrunched under my boots. The sun sent early tree shadows streaking across the silver meadow, and my shadow followed me in the pale light. I could sense the earth breathing slowly, slowly, as if resting after its labors. The midwife farmer had delivered up the fruits of the land, and now the mother lay and slept. Starlings were clattering, moths were busy on the bladder campion in the verges, and I surprised a rabbit that came flying out of a bank of thistles, leaping across the path in a single bound, hind legs fully outstretched and white tail bobbing as it disappeared into undergrowth. The miraculous in the everyday. The beauty of the mundane. "All that matters," says my brilliant friend Miller, turning it around, "is that the miraculous become the norm."

Back on Jade, I kept working with images, pretending that she and I had one skin and that I was carrying full wineglasses in my hands, which I kept soft but strong. Any tension I had was mirrored back to me straightaway in a beautiful illustration of cause and effect, a karmic dynamic with ancient echoes rationalized by Newton when he deduced that for every action there is an equal and opposite reaction. I unlocked my elbows so that my hands could stay still, even in a rising trot. I would pretend that my arms were garden hoses and that water was flowing through them to the bit in Jade's mouth. Imagining my body hollow and breathing right through it, especially into the abdomen, helped me connect with Jade's breathing and body; I tried pretending that I was a Russian doll with all my weight in the base of the body, light in the top in order to drop into the hips and feet, softening the shoulders and releasing the sternum. Or I would see my legs as hanging like an old gate on a broken hinge, loose, while thinking "toes up" rather than "heels down" (this helped me unlock my hips). I allowed my arms to separate from my armpits, and I kept wide across my collarbone. Gradually it became easier to relax my knees away from the saddle, but I still, in the more difficult movements, had a job keeping my knees deep, my heels long, and spreading my toes and not clenching them.

I was sitting on my fluffy cloud, using my buttocks as ice-cream scoops, imagining my legs so long that they touched the ground; these all worked wonders for me when I could hold the focus. I became increasingly aware of how much weaker my left hip was, leading to trouble in the left leg on circles where the definition came so much harder. I would picture the shape of the serpentine before I rode it and occasionally finished with a symmetrical, even line. Jade and I practiced figure eights, sometimes with a transition within them, and large circles with a small circle attached, until we were dizzy. I became more physically fit than I had been for a long time; one day I was in a trot for a full 20 minutes and not out of breath.

It was only when I was not clear that things fell apart. Jade's responses were so direct, so intelligent in the sense of not being interfered with by her own thought processes (what a Zen master!) that in this sense she was teaching me the movements, if I could learn from her. She was better at it all than I was. The more I worked, the more I understood the essence of being there, and that the moment the mind is distracted it falls apart. What a discipline it is to keep the focus, just as in zazen. "Don't be distracted," I wrote to myself in my diary. I needed to maintain a calm, relaxed mind, as in meditation, an attentive, relaxed, concentrated mind so that body and mind were united and could unite me with Jade as if I were an inseparable part of her. This is zazen too.

My body is my thoughts, my thoughts are my body. My thoughts and my body are indivisible, and when I am sitting on Jade's back, her thoughts and my thoughts are linked, her body and my body can become one. I become calm and relaxed, she becomes calm and relaxed. "Sitting quietly, doing nothing, spring comes, and the grass grows by itself." I began to understand the wisdom of doing the least to express the most. My tendency was to rush at things and try to do too many things at the same time. As in life . . . I was all too often "painting legs on the snake," that divine Chinese image for wasting energy.

Like meditation, riding is a heightened state of concentrated awareness wherein one is neither tense nor hurried, and certainly never slack. In a "bad" meditation, you feel sleepy and "drop off." Riding badly, you lose focus and are in danger of literally dropping off. The adorable Zen poet Ryōkan, always ready to laugh at his own folly, knew this condition like we all do:

> *Like a fool, like a dunce*
> *Body and mind completely dropped off.*

Without concentration, action is uninformed, fragmented, unconnected, so our focused mind is a primary source of action. Fragmentation often accompanies age. In youth we were whole; there were no sharp separations until we were fed notions and concepts, which as adults we insist on assuming are absolute truths. We are never whole again until we divest ourselves of this emperor's clothing and become childlike again.

I would arrive home with the smell of horse on my hands and in my clothes, my hair flattened and moist with perspiration. But riding-hat hair didn't bother me at all. I glowed with more than physical heat.

THIRTEEN

interdependence

It was a golden day in mid-September. The fields were dormant, the stubble plowed under. The land lay quiet before the sowing of the winter wheat. A light mist rose off the ground in the morning, obscuring rust-tinged leaves as a low sun struggled through. Plums and apples dropped off heavy trees into the damp grass, and blackberries shone on the bramble.

One of the things I had grown to like most about going riding was that I could walk out the door with no gear, no paraphernalia. My boots, hat, and hairband lived in the car, and I needed no possessions with me apart from keys. I would just change into jodhpurs and sweater and go. Yet there would be, after all this time and always, butterflies in my stomach as

I drove down the winding lanes toward the stables. Here I was an older woman dependent as a child on someone to help me, to protect me at some level, and to guide me through my first hesitant independent moves in the world of horseback riding. Yet when I looked back to a year before, it had seemed inconceivable that I would be schooling a horse on my own. I had come a long way, but I was still, I had to admit to myself, uncomfortable around some of the people with their unsmiling ways. And fear, although considerably diminished, was an ever-present ghost.

Jade and I continued to work as summer faded into autumn. She was benefiting from the practice, becoming more supple, more receptive, and fitter in her body (so was I). Horses gain much from dressage: It improves their balance, tones and strengthens their muscles, and destresses them much as it does humans. If we dance, if we do yoga, we feel rebalanced, energized yet calmer, and the work seemed to have the same effect on Jade. There was, however, a moment one afternoon when she lost her balance as we were riding a wavy line up the side of the school, and she stumbled badly, nearly falling. She regained her balance, but I lost mine. I tumbled into the soft bedding of gravel, hitting my head on the fence on the way down. Jade stopped and looked around at me with a deeply penitent expression. Shaken but unhurt, thanks to my state-of-the-art hat, I scrambled to my feet to retrieve the reins, talking to her to make sure she was all right. She dropped her head and looked at me apologetically, as if to ask the same of me. I stroked her muzzle and led her around the school to calm us both before returning to the mounting block to start again. Horses can say sorry, truly.

This lovely time of early autumn was punctuated by entries in my diary recording moments both good and bad, moments when everything was focused, light, and free, others when I lost concentration and lost Jade at the same time. We spent time practicing tear-drop shapes down the long side of the school, doing canter-trot transitions on a 20-yard circle, and then cantering on a 10-yard circle. There was one particular day when, refreshed after a vacation, my riding felt easy and right; I wasn't trying, I was simply enjoying. Moving from the navel came without thinking by now: I moved my hips fluently with the movement of cantering and felt light in the trunk and shoulders. It was second nature to wrap my legs around Jade's rib cage, keeping my feet still and instructing her from the seat and legs. I began to realize that you can be mindful and concentrated even when you are doing things at high speed. Everything, I pondered to myself, everything is relationship. There is nothing in life that isn't.

The consciousness of interdependence is a sine qua non of

Zen. "Things derive their being and nature by mutual depen-
dence and are nothing in themselves," echo the revelations of
modern physics that the constituents of matter are intercon-
nected, interrelated, and interdependent; that nothing can be
fully understood, in particle physics, as an isolated entity, but
only as an integrated part of a whole. This particle-physics
concept of interconnectedness metamorphosed into an actual
experience on horseback: When my mind was open and alert,
Jade and her rider became as one. We felt things at the same
time, we were dependent on each other yet independent in
ourselves. The distinction between subject and object ceased
to exist. We were both observers and both participants. The
observer is also participant: The ego dissolves and dies quietly
under the influence of this inescapable truth. In the death of
the ego we realize we are not separate, but both individual and
related.

"We shall never understand anything until we have found
some contradictions," wrote Niels Bohr, physicist rather than
Zen master (or perhaps both). What could be more Zen than
the statement that "empty space is curved"? The "wisdom of
not knowing" is verified by the observation that the more accurately you know the position of a particle, the less accurately
you know its velocity. Thus, even if we could have measured
our speed as we galloped across the field, to a billionth of a bil-

lionth of a mile per second, we could have no absolute knowledge of *where* we were at the same time.

There is a core of uncertainty at the heart of things, which
the Zen masters knew before particle physics "discovered" it.
Time is just as enigmatic as space. The distinction between
past, present, and future is only an illusion, according to Ein-
stein. Certainties—there are none. The security of insecurity
is the only security.

As Jade and I practiced our dressage movements and I
watched her strong neck relax and stretch out in front of me,
felt her powerful quarters move under me, I had a sense of her
energy mingling with my energy as if we were part of a continuum of countless molecules and atoms. It was as if there was
no separation and we were just an unending mutation of particles into particles, created from energy and vanishing into
energy. In this rhythm of eternal recycling, what was there to
fear? We became an inseparable energy pattern, a pattern that
is "new in every moment," like every moment of our lives. Interconnectedness, instead of being a concept, became an experience, a realization that it is out of ignorance that we divide
the world that we perceive "out there" into things separate
from ourselves. We are an integrated part of a whole, and this
interconnectedness of all things at each moment highlights the
richness of the present moment. We understand this myste-

rious truth in timeless moments, moments on horseback, or listening to music or hearing great poetry, moments that are torched into the memory, illuminating the understanding.

And what had the late great Miller to say about this? Much, of course; it informed his view on life and how he lived it. His expansive soul and generous nature made the connection all right:

My destiny is linked with that of every other living creature inhabiting this planet—perhaps with those on other planets too, who knows? I refuse to jeopardize my destiny by regarding life within narrow rules that are laid down to circumscribe it. . . . I will try to live my life in accordance with the vision I have of things eternal.

—"Second Letter to Trygve Hirsch"

FOURTEEN

suchness

There is the world. And there is another world—of horses, a world divorced from our everyday world. Stables are usually hidden places, tucked away off the beaten track, set apart from the busy thoroughfares of life. It is fairly seldom that we see horses being ridden on roads and lanes or even across the countryside. Sometimes we see them grazing, usually in pairs or groups, in the fields, heads down at their pretty much full-time activity. (Horses have surprisingly small stomachs for their enormous bulk, designed simply to break down fibers in the food. This food then passes into a 130-foot gut for fermentation, with an appendix 3 feet long to break down the fibrous waste.) But the indoor life of horses is a world apart, and when you go into this other world you step, like Alice, through the looking glass.

It is a world where I met people who are different, who seemed to be living another existence in another life. Looking after horses is labor intensive and time consuming to the extent that those who deal with them have to live in a world apart. Horses do not take days off from needing feeding and being mucked out. There is neither time nor energy for those who look after them to engage with the "outside" world, nor may they want to anyway. They are a tribe with their own dialect. But then horses come from another world too, and we know so little about that wild world. Humans will never have a relationship with them as one horse has with another. The worlds are separate, however much we understand and however close the bond. If you lose contact with that horse-riding world, as I did during the weeks following my accident, the distance increases and the focus is lost. It is a world that feeds on its own intensity.

On first crossing the threshold of the tribe I faced a wall of "them and us." I was definitely "them." Forgetting the Zen wisdom that "the more you talk and think about it, the further you wander from the truth," I spent futile time trying to analyze what "us" meant. In my limited, perhaps unlucky, experience, they were frequently offhand, cold, harsh, and ungracious. Smiles were rare, and welcoming gestures met with indifference. Talking about the psychology of "horsey" people to a Zen vet, she told me that they were notorious in the profession for being difficult (this was an understatement coming from a practitioner who does not care to make judgments about people). In desperation one day, I wrote in my diary, "Does anyone know of a stable run by Buddhists?"

It struck me that perhaps there was something in the collective psyche that needs to project unhappy experiences and feelings on to the psyche of the horse, this giant of patience and tractability who will absorb negativity without protest. Not without harm, though. Horses never forget cruelty. A woman like Madge was clearly wiping her psychological boots on her horses. Such damaged people often inflict their anger and pain on those around them, unaware of what they project onto their horses (let alone their clients). It was a lesson to me in what *not* to do with my own frustration as I disentangled myself from the heavy weight of incompatibility that I lived with. Luckily I had recognized my anger for what it was, a survival strategy that dammed up the deluge of grief that lay behind it.

Riding stables seemed to attract, like bees to the honeypot, people with emotional problems that they could not (or would not) solve and that they dumped on the horses. A friend who runs stables in the United States reckoned that this was a particularly British phenomenon. I hoped so for the sake of horses worldwide. My encounters with these angry people made me angry, and this was not useful. I finally did resort to the advice of Seng-ts'an: "To set up what you like against what you dislike is a disease of the mind. . . . It is due to our choosing to accept or reject that we do not see the true nature of things. . . . Move among and intermingle, without distinction."

There was another, less sinister, interpretation from a friend who had ridden all her life. For some people, she said, caring for horses may fulfill their own need for the care they lacked in their lives, so they project their need for care onto caring for horses. In this way, horses may become a surrogate for those human relationships that have been found to fall short of satisfying. I was in a world of conjecture here, where generalizations were not as useful as insights that might come from my individual experience. It was self-evident to me that there is a relationship factor in horseback riding, but for me it was not a substitute. I was not (I hoped) striking up relationships with all the horses I enjoyed riding because I was/am deficient in human relationships; it is because I *enjoy* the process of a relationship in its different guises. But I could also see that this relationship was immensely important to me at a time when I was struggling to resolve a deadlock in my personal life at home. The mirror of a relationship was being held up, and in it I could see that no person can purify another. The horses brought healing and solace in my grief as well as excitement and challenge as I floundered to celebrate life in its fullness against the pressure of those walls that constricted me.

It may be that for some people, the relative emotional freedom around horses satisfies their particular needs. Compared to a relationship with a dog, who is closely dependent and expressively demonstrative, one with a horse is not so unconditional. A horse is more naked than a dog or a cat. He is more independent of you, more dependent on being one of the herd with his fellow creatures. With horses, you cannot finally be certain of anything because they are high-strung, instinctive animals whose strength has the power to kill, albeit inadvertently. However, although there is not much that can be totally relied upon in a horse (even the most placid shire horse can tread on your foot accidentally and crush it), he may become the best friend you ever had, even to the point where he will give up his life for you.

The converse to the profound degree of understanding that you can achieve with a horse, which is unequaled, is the ever-present element of risk, meaning the ultimate risk of death. This love is a huge gamble, and therein lies an attraction. He looks at you with that wise peripheral eye and seems to know you in a different dimension from the way you know yourself. "I see you, I see you," says Equus to Man in Peter Shaffer's famous play. He is a mirror, and mirrors don't lie. Only *we* lie to our bathroom mirrors, seeing what we want to see. Horses do not allow that. They are what they are and insist that we be who we are. We have walked through the looking glass to find the truth on the other side, and in the stillness of his eye we see "the mirror of heaven and earth, the glass of everything. Emptiness, stillness, tranquility." (Chuang-tzu used both mirrors and horses as metaphors.) We cannot relate to them through direct control, but rather through a dreamlike image of reality that is unintentional, that version of reality that is more real through its intersection with the timeless, yet entirely connected to the present; that disturbs nothing because is is entirely integrated in what it is. "Enlightenment is like the moon reflected on the water. The moon does not get wet, nor is the water broken," wrote the great Dōgen in *The Treasury of the Eye of True Dharma*.

This is an enchanted world behind the looking glass, beyond the reflection, where magic can be found in fleeting, unpredictable moments, where instinctual fears are surmounted, where skills are honed and relationships formed that have an intensity like no other. Its magic ensnared me, engulfing my thinking and feeling and dreaming. I felt sucked into this world every week as I drove across country to my Sunday lessons to the tolling of church bells that drifted over the morning fields. It was the time of the harvest moon, when early mists silence the earth under a light blanket. A sloe tree hung over the gate to the stables, growing out of a hedge, its full, firm fruits showing blue through their dusty bloom. "The world is a mirror of infinite beauty," wrote Thomas Traherne (the 17th-century English writer and Christian mystic) in his *Centuries*. "It is an inestimable joy that I was raised out of nothing to see and enjoy this glorious world."

Like nature in its beauty but also in its terrible power, horses are just what they are. Chuang-tzu wrote,

Horses have hooves so that their feet can grip on frost and snow. They have shaggy hair so they can withstand the cold winds. They eat grass and water, and they like to leap and gallop, because this is their nature. Horses in the wild are content. They show affection for each other by rubbing necks; they show anger by turning their backs and kicking. This is how horses naturally behave.

They embody "suchness," that neutral quality of ordinariness, of "is-ness," that defies definition. It's like trying to define what saltiness is. You come down to the fact that it's salty. Salty is salty, that is its quality, it is just how it is. What is salty? Salty. Taking that a step further, we recognize in "suchness" a state of total acceptance that is unconditional. Everything is as it is. No attitudes, judgments, or any other patterns of conditional thinking and feeling. All it requires is being fully present in the moment. "Life," wrote Henry Miller in a wise moment, "has no other discipline to impose, if we would but realize it, than to accept life unquestioningly." The moments of pure awareness that I experienced while riding Jade, Dulcie, Humphrey, and the others were encounters with suchness: There were no questions or answers, no explanations or justifications, no moralizing or rationalizing. These horses gave me experiences whose essence was of complete freedom of interpretation.

Suchness is experienced by letting go and trusting. It is very ordinary. It is only extraordinary in the sense that we do not see it in all its simplicity most of the time. But it just comes when it comes, natural and obvious; we cannot manufacture it. "A sword cannot cut itself . . . self cannot understand self . . . the way cannot be followed by trying," goes a Zen aphorism. But when it does come, we recognize the ground of our being and the infinitude of our interconnectedness.

The horse has traveled with us across the spectrum of human existence from the folly and tragedy of war to the sublimity of legend. Seeds of wonder at his majestic beauty flower perennially in the human psyche. A cave painting of a galloping horse in the caves of Lascaux is one of the earliest known works of art, and ever since then artists and poets have celebrated the horse's nobility and power. When the Christian cavalry appeared in the New World, the natives thought that horse and rider were one person—an interesting perception in the light of the Zen of riding, except that they took them for gods. Horses have been and still are companions, friends, and helpers of those who choose to care for them, in spite of centuries of sacrifice in war.

Here the statistics speak of carnage that is unimaginable, except that it actually happened. During the 2,000 days of World War II, 865 horses were killed every day. The Red Army used between 3 million and 5 million horses, and at the Battle of Stalingrad alone, 52,000 German horses were lost. The same number were shot by German soldiers on orders from headquarters before they retreated defeated from the Crimea. They used 14 million horses in the course of World War I, and the British, who used draft horses to draw the cannon, lost over a quarter of a million animals. Of the half-million horses engaged in the Boer War, 150,000 did not survive. The Wild West was won on the backs of tough, strong horses, but no figures exist to count the casualties.

Horses are still used to work the land in underdeveloped countries, and for those where technology and mechanization have taken over, the horse now finds his place in sport, hunting, racing, dressage, and leisure-time riding. He provides physiotherapy for the sick, therapeutic riding for the disabled, and hippotherapy for the psychologically disturbed. For blind people, riding can be a uniquely emotional experience, and horses have even been able to help those with behavioral and social problems. The how of it defies definition, and the experience often transcends words. In this it is perfectly Zen.

FIFTEEN

equilibrium
and balance

By now I was thinking seriously about renting or sharing a horse. In my flightier moments, I had considered buying my own, keeping her in a friend's field near the village or in a local livery, and refocusing my life around looking after her, riding her, and spending my spare time enjoying the relationship. But in my more realistic moments, I could see that not only was the commitment too great (a daily one that would be difficult if not impossible to tie in with my writing, teaching, and home life, creating more tension than already existed), but it also was prohibitively expensive. I made inquiries about full-time and half-time livery and about do-it-yourself livery, and came to the conclusion that I was in the wrong income bracket.

Maybe owning a horse was not that high a priority, I persuaded myself. Taking a share in a horse was a real possibility, though. Paying a reasonable sum every month along with another person, I could ride a livery horse at Rushbrook (or elsewhere) by arrangement with them—probably three or four times a week, and visit at any time. Pippa suggested that I take a share in Fly; her owner was looking for a riding partner. Excited, I went to see her in her stable to see if I could kindle a spark between us, but the chemistry was not there. It never had been. Tossing her lackluster head from side to side over the stable door, she gave me a sour look. My instinct told me that it would be a waste of time. I wondered about Jade, because to share her would be a dream come true, but someone had beaten me to it and was riding her whenever her owner, Helen's husband, couldn't. Humphrey was too big and strong for me to handle on my own out hacking and was not a dressage horse, anyway, and I definitely wanted to continue my work in the school. Helen offered me a look at Oats, a handsome dark chocolate-colored hunter standing just under 17 hands tall, but again he was too big and strong, not a dressage horse, and in any case was lame that day, which did not seem a good omen. I sensed that I was not experienced enough for him and that his favorite thing was dashing across the countryside jumping fences and ditches. I was going to have to wait patiently until the right horse presented itself.

Meanwhile, the hunting season was starting and Jade was busy, so I started having lessons on Hermann, an 11-year-old chestnut thoroughbred. Hermann was a darling; he was good-natured in the dozey way of the slightly dim. He had belonged to a gentleman in his eighties who had kept him in livery at Rushbrook and had ridden until the day of his death (by natural causes). The gentleman had left his horse to Helen in his will. Hermann was an orphan and needed riders. He seemed quietly, sweetly resigned to his destiny. He lived tucked away behind the tack room in a stable that was dark and poky, with an old-fashioned manger on the wall. He was nibbling hay from it as we unbolted the door and turned his head to look at us. We were interesting enough for him to stop eating, and I patted his neck as Pippa removed his blanket. I could see neat rows of bridles hanging up beyond his stable door, saddles on saddle racks, halters hung from huge hooks. The smell of newly polished leather merged with the tobacco sweetness of Hermann's hay. He had a long head with a white star on his forehead, hazel eyes, and a rich chestnut mane that fell over the muscles of his neck.

The liquid light of late September poured into the school as we warmed up, walking around the perimeter fence to get used to each other. Pippa, her fair hair plaited to the back of her head and a woollen scarf around her neck, hugged herself to keep warm as she walked up and down in the center, calling out instructions. The pear tree in the stable yard was heavy with fruit, spotlit by the low sun, and a brackish smell rose from the damp earth beneath it. Hermann had a rambling walk that verged on the laid-back. He needed encouragement to stay awake and keep going forward through the soft gravel, but was receptive enough to my encouragement. I was feeling the unbearable sadness of life that day, and possibly my low-key mood transmitted to him. But his trot had a bounce to it that took me by surprise and raised my tempo, and the rest of the lesson was spent adjusting myself to the movement of this new horse. Because I hadn't ridden him before, he showed up all my faults, particularly my weak left hip. He too was less supple on the left side, so it was doubly hard to achieve equilibrium. I performed some execrable transitions, and the circles were awful. This did not do much to lift my gloom. I felt like an amateur, heavy, unskillful, and unhappy. Pippa, who must have sensed my pessimism, was sweetly encouraging.

"It's the best thing for you at this point," she said. "You and Jade were getting to know each other very well and things were going brilliantly, but you have to ride other horses, too, to learn more about your riding."

I knew she was right, but I just didn't want to know. I wanted to be on Jade's familiar back and continue with our work. I didn't want to start again; it felt too difficult. I remembered feeling like this in my childhood, rebellious and miserable, and found myself indulging in an old habit of judging myself harshly for being so pathetic. My inner state of disequilibrium was mirrored by my dysfunctional riding at that point in the lesson. "Remember," I told myself, "outer balance can only come from inner balance." It was a timely reminder that Zen is a process—like life, it is moving and changing every moment. "Put down the garbage of the past and future and come back to the present," I told myself. "Be like a child again, innocent and empty." For the rest of the lesson, I suspended my judgments, allowed myself to experience the feelings of difficulty and become myself in the present moment. "When you are you, you see things as they are, and you become one with your surroundings." How true it was that day, riding Hermann, experiencing the eminently ordinary event of being myself, warts and all.

Once again a mirror was being held up. Mirrors grasp nothing, refuse nothing, receive anything, but retain nothing, reflecting back to us as much as we want to see. However, the ultimate mirror is difficult to escape. Dōgen, in his inimitable prose, wrote that "the whole moon and the entire sky are reflected in dewdrops on the grass, or even in one drop of water." He taught that mind and body are one, yet embraced the paradox that they are also two. Not two, not one, yet both two and one. When we have our body and mind in order, everything else will exist in the right place and in the right way. The body cannot relax until the mind is relaxed, and this is just as true for the horse as it is for the rider.

Horses need to meditate and daydream too, which is why they benefit from leisurely walks in the countryside, just as we do. The master of classic riding, Udo Burger, taught that good performance always depends on relaxation:

> *The first thing that a rider must learn, if he aims to become an artist, is the art of relaxation. This means detachment, serenity, enjoyment of work for the sake of beauty, unconcern with success or failure, praise or criticism . . . Total harmony of movement between the two bodies is the essence of the art . . . He must learn to meditate whenever he is given the opportunity to relax, to loosen excessive mental or physical tension. No valuable work can be produced without thought.*
>
> —The Way to Perfect Horsemanship

I began to relax my hands, relax my legs, and to give the lesson the concentration I had been denying it. "No goals, no expectations," I told myself. And what happened? I began to ride in lightness, to balance without tension as Hermann's gait became more familiar. This relaxation, in the sense of total concentration of the mind on the senses, was, I could now understand, essential to the art of riding. Then and only then could the moment of the experience be undifferentiated, when there is no awareness of division between horse and rider. The horse is me, I am the horse, in perfect equilibrium that comes only from a condition of unselfconscious awareness, and the acceptance of "suchness." I was, after my storm of inner protest, consenting to collaborate with what was, and the result was equilibrium.

The following Sunday, I had an early morning lesson at a time when most of the world is still asleep, or, at most, reading the paper over a cup of coffee. The first frost was thick on the car, the sky clear and bright with a low sun lighting up autumn leaves on the trees. I helped Pippa tack up Hermann in his little stable which, due to be mucked out while I rode him, smelt deliciously of straw and manure. She was the worse for wear after a late night drinking with friends, and while we removed Hermann's blanket and saddled and bridled him I heard the story of her evening. Looking at her bleary eyes, I felt guilty for getting her up so early, but was glad for my own clear head as I mounted Hermann and walked him across the yard. The fine gravel of the schooling ring was crisp with cold.

"I was watching Grace ride the other day," I told Pippa as

she followed me in. "She was in a local dressage competition, and I was impressed with how still she kept her feet. Could we work on that?"

So we did. It was a simple lesson, for which I was grateful, just concentrating on this one element of many. Accustoming myself to Hermann's trot again, with its springy action, was difficult enough, let alone keeping my feet still and quiet and allowing my hips to make the movement. I began to understand that balance is really an *act* of balancing. It is a dynamic process, not a static state, a process of continual change that is always adjusting to the shifting flow of circumstances (as on horseback, so in life). Once it becomes instinctive, it is experienced as a stillness in the center of movement. The eye of the storm. Hermann moved more freely under me once I identified my center of balance in my abdomen and started to move from my navel. This balanced us, connected us, and established the polarity of gravity and lightness, rootedness into my feet, and space in my trunk. When it worked it felt sublimely simple.

The "still point of the dance" is that cultivated stillness in the center of all change that keeps balance regardless of circumstance. The active stillness of equanimity and equilibrium. Everyone has this balance. It is only a matter of attention, and this is what Zen brings to life. In balancing, you have two legs, and the two legs give you the oneness of balance. Equilibrium does not exist outside the moment of balance. Balance, both physical and mental, is an instant and spontaneous adjustment to unfolding events, and the remembering of the freedom of living within the boundaries of your own nature. It is the full acceptance of every instant, every moment. It is unconsidered and spontaneous; it happens without one thought of what to do. It is the still point around which everything moves. When I kept my feet still and allowed the movement forward and up- ward from the hips, yet grounded into the heels, then I felt the beauty of this stillness, this balance. The trouble was, the mo- ment I thought about it, it fell apart. Pippa couldn't help laughing when it did, and joining in the mirth, I quoted her one of my favorite Zen poems, one of the few that I know by heart:

> *The centipede was happy quite*
> *Until a toad in fun*
> *Said, "Pray which leg comes after which?"*
> *This worked his mind to such a pitch,*
> *He lay distracted in a ditch*
> *Considering how to run.*

She loved it. I drove home happy in spite of the failures and walked on air for the rest of the day.

SIXTEEN

"this" is also "that"

That evening I lit a bonfire. The garden was ready to be put to bed for the winter, and a huge pile of seedheads, branches, weeds, and clippings needed burning. At sunset, the sky made an enormous bruise around the raw wound of the sun. I stood back and watched smoke curl up into the trees behind the garden fence; a moth crept across the grass as the light faded. In a secluded corner at the top of the garden, I communed with life and nature as it burned. That evening, there was no wind, and clouds of midges hovered in the damp garden. I love the smell of the bonfire, the activity, the sound of it as it crackles and sizzles and hisses and sends thick, white clouds of smoke drifting over the field. The art of the bonfire is, first of all, getting a hot heart at the center, then knowing when to turn it, when to stack it up, how much wet stuff to put on and when, when to gather up stray branches from the bottom and around the edge to pile onto the middle and feed it, and how to prevent it from burning too freely so that it devours itself. I was absorbed and happy, tending the fire until it burnt itself out, still crackling into the nighttime as the dark trees watched the stars come out.

The following Tuesday I had my first session alone on Hermann in the school. I had come from an almost sleepless night of despair about where to turn and what to do about my disintegrating relationship with my partner—and how to do it. Riding Hermann made me feel a whole lot better; it healed the pain and soothed the tumult of my mind. I talked to him as we worked in transitions and circles, gradually getting to know him. I began to harmonize with his movement in trot, rising from my heels and moving my hips in suppleness. It was made harder by his habit of tossing his head, an unbalancing action for the rider, and when we went into a canter I found it difficult to be relaxed and easy in the saddle. I wrapped my legs around his slender body, squeezing with calves rather than using my feet to urge him on, and opened my knees to loosen my hips, finding immediately that I could swing into the movement of the canter as well as rising and sitting trots, with more grace. I experimented with sinking my center of gravity on the in-breath as my diaphragm flattened, and found him more responsive and less likely to toss his head. I began to talk to him with soft hands rather than yanking him to keep straight. I tried a few transitions without stirrups, from a walk to a trot, and had fleeting moments of staying right down in the legs and sitting deep rather than being bounced out of the saddle.

I found that because his twist from left to right was similar to my own, riding Hermann accentuated the difference between my right- and left-side flexibility. This was not a comfortable experience. What it showed up was my pronounced twist to the left, which made my right shoulder come forward. I needed to open it back, drop the left hip, stretch up the left side of the trunk and sink down into the heel in order to be balanced. Having to think about this and work out how to deal with it interfered with the "letting go" that I needed to cultivate. It was too easy for me to lapse into judgment and self-criticism and forget that setting up what you like against what you dislike is a disease of the mind, and that it is due to our choosing to accept or reject that we do not see the true nature of things. By doing so we set up difference and division, which are the opposite of harmony. I had not yet understood that these two are opposite sides of the same coin. Polarized they may be, but poles are connected through the center, and if I could stay in that middle place and let go of my "judgmental" side, I would understand that "this" and "that" cease to be opposites. Sandokai said:

> Light and darkness oppose each other
> Yet the one depends on the other
> As the stepping of the right leg on the stepping of the left.

The dawning of this realization felt like a homecoming. The *unio mystica*—a sense of unity with the divine, experienced in states of rapture or absorption—in Zen terms means exactly that, coming home, because everything that exists lives undemandingly from the center of being, without having left it or being able to leave it. So in order to live from the center, like Hermann did so spontaneously, I would have to negate everything in me that is off center: not just my physical imbalance, but also my judgmental mind. People who are centered can do anything and go anywhere because they perceive the universal harmony inherent in all things, even in the middle of great pain. They have found peace in their hearts. Judgments about "this" and "that" are superfluous: "easy gives rise to difficult, after follows before." Suspending judgment in unconditional acceptance leaves a state of grace, a state of perfect equilibrium that leaves us wanting for nothing. In this wisdom, the Zen master adapts to the circumstances of the present moment so that he is in harmony with his environment: Rather than force change on himself, he adapts to the movement of life. The 13th-century German mystic Eckhart said that "the eye with which I see God is the same eye with which God sees me." It struck me as the same mystic experience of the Zen archer, where fundamentally the marksman aims at himself.

All this because of my right shoulder. I was repeatedly amazed at how mundane facts or everyday events were teaching me profound truths. By teaching me to accept fate, they facilitated my feeling fully alive. This great surrender induced a calmness, trusting that everything that is, is there because it has its place. It's called collaborating with the inevitable. I didn't have to go into psychoanalysis or to a monastery to learn this (although the latter would have been lovely). Whatever my life setting, it appeared, the perennial wisdom was available, in every moment of my ordinary life. I am my own bedrock, I do not need to seek elsewhere. It is all here, now, and both past and future are contained in this "now."

"Maybe," I thought to myself, "maybe Hermann is the horse I should take a share in. He is the right age—not too young and fizzy, nor too old and slow." At 16 hands, he was the right size (I liked riding bigger horses), and if he had a vice it was that he was rather lazy—but that was erring on the right side as far as a novice like me was concerned. He was good to school because we had similar faults and could help correct each other. There it was, an opportunity in front of me and I had failed to see it. I was, to quote the Zen adage, "the man who rides the donkey in search of the donkey he is riding." I decided to book him for some solitary hacks, to go out on my own with him and see how it felt together. I was exhilarated by the idea. It felt like the first day of winter, a stunning day of windy skies, bronze oaks, and dramatic clouds. I drove home into a blinding sun that silhouetted forests and fields against the evening sky.

I arranged to take Hermann out the following week. It was a cold November day, and the wind whistled around my cottage. Raindrops hit the window panes like glass on glass, spasmodically blown around by blustery gusts. I wondered whether to cancel, and called Helen for reassurance.

"I'm a bit concerned about the wind," I said. "It might spook him. Do you think it's a good idea, or should I take him out when the weather has settled?"

"No, don't worry about a thing," said Helen. "It'll be fine. He's been out in worse. You'll be all right."

Hermann was out in the field with several other horses. I

collected his halter from the tack room and squelched my way across the soggy grass to catch him. No problem: A single carrot did the trick. He thanked me with a little snuffle. Dragging my boots through the mud, I led him back to the stable, his head nodding at my shoulder to the rhythm of his walk. I could feel his warm breath on my neck. The concrete in the yard had been hosed down and swept clean, and as I walked past the line of stables I could hear hooves rustling in the straw and the sound of munching as the other horses crunched their oats out of their lunch buckets. I clumsily tacked Hermann up singlehandedly, my fingers frozen, and led him out to the mounting block. Helen was standing nearby talking to a trainer, and when she saw me she came over.

"You've done up the girth on the wrong buckle," she pointed out. "It's all twisted."

She wrestled with it but couldn't undo it. I felt sheepish. She called the trainer to come and help, and together they managed to sort it out. Feeling truly small, I mounted, attempting to maintain a dignified smile, thanked her, and set off. It was a bad start.

The wind was still gusting around ferociously, and it was cold. We walked up a narrow lane and crossed to a grassy footpath. Hermann splashed his way through several enormous puddles onto a stretch of waterlogged ground still soaked by last night's rain. His hooves glooped through the squelching mud, slipping and sliding alarmingly. I talked to him intermittently to keep him calm. He was tossing his head and seemed jumpy, reacting to the movement of the tangled trees. I felt as tense and nervous as he did, however consciously I tried to relax. Once we got out into open country he did not want to move, so at most we had some leisurely trots, under seeming duress from him. Neither of us was enjoying it.

I took a short, circular route. I sighed with relief when we turn toward home, and Hermann's pace picked up. We emerged back into the tiny lane where we had started our ride and were about 300 yards from the stable when a paper bag blew into the road. Hermann stopped. He would not walk past it. I cajoled him, reassured him, scolded him, tried silence, and kicked him on, but nothing worked. He would not go past that paper bag. After 10 minutes I was becoming desperate. There was no other way to the stables, at least not one that was less than several miles. It would have been worse to have dismounted to try to lead him past, in case he refused and bolted. I turned him around to face away from the paper bag and, holding the reins with one hand and praying that no traffic would come shooting around the corner, fumbled for my mobile phone. I dialed the stables. Humiliating as it would be, I would ask one of the stable girls to come out and remove the paper bag. The phone rang. And rang. There was no answer. Nobody was in the office. I kept calling. No answer.

Swallowing a lump in my throat, I put the phone back in my pocket. My heart was pounding. At that moment a Range Rover came into view from up the road. I waved to the driver to stop. He opened his window and I leaned forward over Hermann's neck.

"I am really, really sorry to ask you this, but my horse is spooked by that paper bag and he will not go past it. Would you mind moving it for me? I would be so grateful. I'm truly sorry to have to bother you."

Luckily, he succumbed to my entreaty. Perhaps he saw desperation in my face. He drove slowly past us and, clambering out of his stylish car, gingerly picked up the filthy paper bag. He took care to hide it in the hedge before driving on. I waved and called thanks. It was nice of him. I was lucky.

We walked quietly home, my nerves shot and my body numb from the piercing wind. It would be quite a while until I felt ready to go out on my own again.

SEVENTEEN

making your own destiny

As the days began to darken, my routine Sunday morning lessons continued, and I also took Hermann into the school to practice once a week. Meanwhile, I was still hacking out regularly with my sister on Dulcie, riding across open countryside as the season changed from fall to winter. Dulcie's cold-weather coat grew thick and dark, and grooming her was warm work, especially when she had taken a roll in the mud. When I finished, I would stroke the pale, down-soft patch between her nostrils and she would lower her long-lashed eyes and coyly submit to the caress before I led her to the upturned milk crate that served as our mounting block.

One Sunday, I arrived as usual at Rushbrook for my lesson,

but Pippa was nowhere to be seen. My warm breath made mist in the frosty air as I made my way across from Hermann to Jade's stable to see if she was there. Nobody was around, and the tack room was locked. It was a crystal day at the end of November with a clear, pale sky and bare trees, although a few still had their autumn leaves. I jumped up and down to keep warm and was just returning to my car for shelter when I saw Pippa turn into the drive. She parked her car and got out.

"Sorry I'm late. I've just been talking to Helen, and she says that you can ride Leo today."

"Leo?"

"Yes, Leo is Helen's new horse. He's in the stable next to Jade. He's a youngster, about 6 years old, and she is training him for the Burleigh Horse Trials. He's beginning to respond really well to dressage."

I had noticed Leo while practicing in the school, because he had been busy wrecking his stable door for the past 2 weeks. Two new doors had had to be fixed already. So this was Leo.

Pippa and I tacked him up together, removing his blanket and fixing him up with a martingale. He was a bright-eyed gelding, enthusiastic and lively with a lithe, well-toned body. Youth emanated from every pore. He gave off the feeling that he was about to take off at any moment. He had a glossy chestnut coat, and his mane was auburn blond. This gorgeous creature was slim and long legged, with a shapely head and well-muscled quarters. We led him, unwilling, swishing his tail and skipping, to the mounting block, where he decided to dance and play. In the end, we used another set of stone steps in the center of the yard where he could be prevailed on to stand still just long enough for me to mount. He walked toward the dressage school, and immediately I felt the elastic spring and energy of a young horse, which was completely different from the relaxed gait of Hermann and the rolling amble of Jade. Leo felt alive through and through.

He was extremely sensitive to any movement I made, even the tiniest nuance. If I tightened, he tightened; if I relaxed, he relaxed. Writ large. For the first time I had the experience of feeling what "on the bit" means. Both Jade and Hermann and perhaps all the others, too, had been toughened by age and repeated riding, and were relatively deadened in the mouth. Here was a young horse who had not been broken in long, who was still new to the game, willing to learn and respond. As we worked he began to stretch out his neck and lower his head to come into perfect balance. My hands became quiet, soft, in response to his sensitive mouth. Leo was as supple as elastic, responding to my aids instantaneously, and he gave me moments of lightness in balance, and a feeling of being in control as I moved with him. This was a totally new experience.

"Well done!" said Pippa as we finished. "That went really well. And I have to say I felt uncertain about you riding him, about how it would go, because you haven't ridden such a young horse before, and he is incredibly sensitive—and can be very frisky. Let's have another go on him in a few weeks and maybe try a canter."

Words cannot describe how I felt that day. I simply wrote in my diary, "I would rather be doing this than anything else on earth."

The second time I rode Leo, Pippa sent me off to mount him on my own while she dealt with another pupil. I led him to the stone steps, and after several abortive attempts to get him into position, to still his dance long enough for me to scramble into the saddle, I made it. But he continued dancing, and I did the wrong thing. I tightened the reins and gripped with my knees. He nearly took off and would have bolted if one of the other teachers had not been nearby and seen what was happening.

"Soften your legs!" he yelled. "Now bring them forward." I did.

Helen joined in from the top of the yard. "Loosen the reins," she shouted. They both came over and helped to calm Leo.

"That's one of the things that he can't stand," said Helen.

"Any feeling of tightness when you first get on his back makes him want to bolt. Stay relaxed and he'll be relaxed."

I had learned my lesson. Learned the paradox that by relaxing and letting go I was far more likely to stay on than if I tried to stay on by gluing myself to his back and hanging onto the reins. Even if I fell off, it was better to be relaxed than tight; I would hurt myself less. I breathed myself down. We rode carefully and steadily into the school and began the lesson.

I concentrated on a soft opening of my hips, sitting well down into the saddle like into a deep sofa so that it came up to me. Using the magic of the talking hands, I began to tune in to this delightful horse. A wind had come up and was whistling around the walls of the indoor school, and this unsettled him, but I managed to keep him calm and steady with my voice. We worked both in trot and in canter, Pippa calling instructions against the wind: "Let it happen! Let the horse do the moving! Relax."

Evidently I had not let go enough; I had brought the fear with me from the yard to the school.

"Your main problem," she said, "is that you are still too busy. You move your legs around too much, you try to *do* too much. You don't have to do much at all. Less is more."

I understood this in my head, but translating it into action was still another matter. "As in life," I thought to myself wryly.

"Think of the parts behind your hand as a well-strung bow, elastic but also firmly braced. One end of the bow is at the withers, and it extends over the neck and poll, being fixed at the other end to his mouth and to the bit, which is connected back to the hands by the reins."

After that it went better: I decided to adopt my mode of "I don't care." With the image of the bow in mind, I unlocked my hips as we cantered, letting go of myself and allowing Leo freedom of gait as I followed his movement with my seat. For the first time in a long time, my hands managed to stay still, while the strung bow controlled him lightly on the bit. I found my lower leg sitting back more naturally, bringing me to a feeling of easy balance. There were moments when I felt totally aware of everything that was happening in Leo, in myself, and in my surroundings, an intense wakefulness that filled my whole body.

The awareness that came with this wakening was that if I willed something with my mind, it could happen. But I had to make it happen, I couldn't just expect the horse to do it undirected. "Luminous is the mind, brightly shining," said the Buddha, and this power of the mind, intrinsically connected with the body as it is, forges our destinies. "We are what we think: All that we are arises with our thoughts. With our thoughts, we make the world," (the Buddha again). My destiny is thus of my own making. Only my own negativity is an impediment, the spirit of negation whom I know as my personal Mephistopheles. "Your own enemy cannot harm you as much as your own thoughts, unguarded. But once mastered, no one can help you as much, not even your mother or your father." In the end, I had to come back to myself: It had to be *me*, doing what I thought I had to do without trying to follow anybody else's pattern. Every single human being is unique and has his own life to live. As the Zen aphorism goes, "If you do not get it from yourself, where will you get it from?"

EIGHTEEN

right practice

Riding Leo brought home to me an ancient truth, one I was already familiar with through yoga. That is that artistry in any medium is a combination of talent, application, and hard work. The great geniuses are always at work. Whatever degree of accomplishment you may achieve in your chosen field, it is the fruit of practice. To ride well would require of me, just as it had in yoga, a wholehearted discipline of regular work. It was up to me. Nobody else could do it for me. I could set my sights on anything and achieve it if I followed it up with consistent, mindful practice. In that practice alone would come true understanding. Henry Miller, urging me on as always, wrote that "today I see that my steadfast desire was alone responsible for whatever progress or mastery I have made. The reality is always there, and it is preceded by vision. And if one keeps looking steadily, the vision crystallizes into fact or deed." I believed it.

I was riding three or sometimes four times a week during that winter, heeding Miller's advice that "everything involves time and discipline. You must practice regularly or you lose out. You have to be it and do it every day; that is one of the reasons why a man like Picasso is so marvelous. He never loses his touch because he is constantly at it." The yoga master Vivekenanda said that there is only one sin, and that is the sin of weakness: "be strong" was his advice. The way forward was to demand much of myself and expect little of others: My life was of my own making, the creation of my mind. It is the readiness of the mind that is wisdom.

There were days when it felt too difficult, when I felt I was getting nowhere and had to bring myself firmly back to the present moment and cheer myself with the Zen thought that to go eastward 1 mile is to go westward 1 mile. There were days when my feet and fingers were frozen and I wished wholeheartedly to be at home on the sofa with a book, preferably one by Henry Miller telling me to enjoy every moment and take life as it comes. "What difference," he asks, "does it make whether you accomplish it today, next week, or next month?" In the end, it was the pure enjoyment of being on horseback and the sweetness of the horses themselves that urged me not to give up. The problems I encountered I took to be "the manure of experience," which hopefully would enrich whatever progress I might make and teach me to turn disappointment into something positive. During the long, dark evenings by the fire, I resorted to my diary and noted many words of the wise concerning practice.

"The law of the universe dictates that peace and harmony can only be won by inner struggle. The little man does not want to pay the price for that kind of peace and harmony; he wants it ready-made, like a suit of manufactured clothes," wrote Miller the tailor's son. There is a Tibetan prayer that asks for "appropriate difficulties and suffering on this journey" in order to become fully awakened, recognizing that very often what nourishes our lives most deeply is what brings us face-to-face with our limitations and the consequent difficulties that arise. "Through dedication and devotion," wrote Henry Miller, "one achieves another kind of victory. I mean the ability to overcome one's problems, not meet them head on." The value of practice in the riding would lead, I hoped, to an increasing ease in making difficult things look simple, indeed making them simple.

"Struggle," he goes on, "is the most valuable experience of all. . . . As long as we are alive we are growing. . . . No end, no conclusion, no completion, perpetual becoming. . . . We should find perfect existence through imperfect existence, perfection in imperfection." In this, he echoed the wisdom of Zen, where practice is seen not as separate from ordinary life, but as an intrinsic part of it. So much so, in fact, that "to practice" can be a self-defeating process, an exercise in futility: The Zen monk Bankei said it is like wiping off blood with blood. The "path to enlightenment" is embodied in all human activity, the whole of life is enlightenment if we are awake. The practice is in every moment. Thus, no one is enlightened and no one is unenlightened. We see into our own nature by bringing light to each act of our existence. Zen is simply to be completely alive. Which is how I felt when I was riding.

The paradox of practice and no-practice intrigued me. I often found, and it was the same with yoga, that when I had a break from it, the first experience afterward was often spectacularly better than when I had been hard at it for weeks. The no-practice was in a sense a form of practice (although obviously there is a fine line between this and sleepy indifference). Somewhere in the depths of the mind, some assimilation was happening, an unseen mental rehearsal that would bear unexpected fruit. Zen connects this inner world of consciousness with the outer world of form, whether it is dealt with directly or indirectly. How it connects with it is through mindfulness, that energy that is prepared for anything, and that sheds light on all things and all activities, awakening the power of concentration and often leading to insight. The practice of mindfulness itself develops that readiness of the mind that is wisdom.

In which case, I wondered, what about zazen, the time-honored practice of Zen meditation? I turned to the masters for clarification. I started with Dōgen. In his *Recommending Zazen to All People*, he wrote:

> . . . *think not-thinking . . . [go] beyond thinking. This is the art of zazen. . . . It is not learning meditation. It is simply the dharma gate of enjoyment and ease. . . . Once you experience it you are like a dragon swimming in the water or a tiger reposing in the mountains. . . .*
>
> *If the slightest discrimination occurs, you will be lost in confusion. . . . Let go of all involvements and let myriad things rest. Do not think good or bad. Do not judge right or wrong. Stop conscious endeavor and analytic introspection. Do not try to become a buddha.*

The practice of sitting still is the direct expression of our true nature, like a reflection in a mirror. But then, conversely (there's always a "conversely" in Zen), Hui-neng points out that any reflection of one's nature is meditation. Sitting can release the sitter into the spontaneity and freedom of just being. Its simplicity is wonderful. It is not about control; it is, rather, a release of control in order to reach an inner stillness that allows things to be as they are. Thoughts come and go without interference until they stop. The avoidance of effort, wu-wei, is intrinsic. Insight may come in the stopping, and the insight itself, the understanding, is also the practice. Zazen does not work if it is purposeful, intentional. It is simply a device, it is not an end itself. It is not leading "somewhere." There are warnings in Zen literature that prolonged and repetitive sitting is not much better than being dead. The Zen scholar Alan Watts wrote, "There is, of course, a proper place for sitting—along with standing, walking, and lying—but to imagine that sitting contains some special virtue is 'attachment to form.' Zazen is not distinguishable from any other activity as a means to enlightenment."

Hui-neng said that "to concentrate the mind on quietness is a disease of the mind, and not mind at all." In the *Platform Sūtra*, he says that the term "sitting" is not limited to physical sitting but refers to a practice where the mind is not influenced or disturbed by anything that arises, internally or in the environment. "Zen," he taught, "is seeing into one's nature, and not of practicing meditation or obtaining liberation." It is grounded in the real world of concrete experience.

"To try to purify the mind is to be contaminated by purity," wrote Alan Watts. We live in the world, in our bodies, just as they are, and the only freedom that has any meaning is to acquire a new consciousness, to have a new view beyond our conditioning. This is what Krishnamurti called "freedom from the known." Henry Miller, ever straining to break through these prison walls, had the experience that "when each thing is lived through to the end, there is no death and no regrets, neither is there a false springtime; each moment lived pushes open a greater, wider horizon from which there is no escape save living." The idea that enlightenment, or salvation, can come as much through fully enjoying pleasure as through the sacrifices of discipline reconciles the way of affirmation with the way of negation, the practice of austerity with the acceptance of life's revelatory richness. "Practice-realization," said Dōgen, "is not defiled with specialness; it is matter for every day." With these words I returned refreshed, every day, to my riding.

NINETEEN

no " I "

I was still looking for a horse to share. My solitary ride with Hermann had not done much to convince me that he was right for me, and riding Leo had highlighted Hermann's deficiencies as far as dressage was concerned. Hermann was not balletic, nor was he particularly interested. Added to that, the number of bridle paths for hacking out around Rushbrook as limited, so countryside rambles were restricted and involved a high ratio of road riding that did not appeal to me. Maybe I would have to look elsewhere. As I talked to Grace about it one day as we traveled back from a yoga seminar, she came up with an idea.

"I've no idea whether this might do for you, but there is a horse up at High Chimneys Farm who is looking for a ride. Why don't you come and see him?"

I quizzed her. He was a 17.3 black gelding with a white star, 7 years old, whose owner had lost interest and who desperately needed exercise. His name was Louis. He was lonely. Grace said she would talk to Maureen, who ran the stables, and find out whether I could come and look at him. I felt excited at the prospect: The countryside around High Chimneys Farm was glorious, and there were numerous bridle-path circuits that hardly used roads at all. Christmas was looming, so it was unlikely that this would happen for a couple of weeks, but I was content with dreaming meanwhile.

New Year's Day dawned like spring under a blue sky strewn with gentle strands of white cloud, the sun slanting pale light over bare trees and hedges. Remembering our ride on the same day the previous year, I called my sister and we arranged to go out on Dulcie and Tandy. It was a beautiful ride where I relaxed right down into the saddle and moved with her, my hands still, my neck free. I practiced the tall, light spine, the open relaxed shoulders, and did the spruce tree and ice-cream legs dribbling around her sides. Three long canters later, I felt serenely at one with the world, and recalled Henry Miller's paean to life: "There's only one life, and it is always good. . . . Life is energy, tremendous energy. . . . It's almost a question of health, of wellbeing. To be healthy is to keep a living current flowing. Vital energy, that's what life is."

I arranged to meet Grace at the stables one Thursday afternoon to have a look at Louis. The memory remains imprinted. I walked into a small courtyard that had three stables on each side, and our eyebeams crossed. Several horses were visible, and I had no idea which was Louis, but I was drawn to him like a magnet. His wistful face looked over the stable door, imploring, "Love me, love me." I couldn't help myself. He was as black as soot, shiny, young and slim, and enormously tall. I had to go up on to tiptoe to stroke the white star on his forehead. I would, I thought, practically need a ladder to get up on his back. Here was a gentle giant, responsive to affectionate hands and a loving voice. He was ridiculously leggy, and I had to stand on a box to put the bridle on. Despite his massive size, I wanted to cuddle him. Grace introduced me to Maureen, a neat, efficient girl with a raven-black bob and fringe. She had large, green eyes and a wide mouth. Briskly, she agreed to give me a short lesson on him. We led him into the school so that she had a chance to assess my riding.

He felt beautiful to ride, in the same way as Leo with that life force of youth but also with an intrinsic balance and grace. I learned some useful tips from Maureen about keeping my hands lower, almost down to his neck, and how to bring him into outline, fingers soft yet firm. "Hold the reins like sponges," she said. With the reins fairly short, the outer rein firm and

155

still, pulling my elbow back on the inside rein to get his attention so that he would lower his head, he came into balance. It all began to work beautifully. Louis responded quickly to the aids from the inside leg to the outside rein and began to stretch out his neck and lengthen his stride. Just as Pippa had done, Maureen noticed that I rushed into things, trying to do too many things at the same time (this familiar habit I recognized in other areas of my life) and talked to me about organizing myself first before changing pace or direction. "Slow down! Take your time!" she called.

She told me to keep my head up and look forward, rather than dropping my chin and looking down, a fault I found difficult to correct. I gradually got the feeling of working him from the quarters, using my calf muscles more in directing him, and going deep into my heels in order to relax my hips. She told me to divide the body into three: "The knees down to the feet do one thing, the hands do another, and the trunk yet another." Maureen was a successful dressage competitor at county level, and she succeeded in making me feel small and uncertain. "One great thing about riding," I wrote in my diary that evening, "is that it is a potent ego reducer."

Like all horses, Louis had no sense of self-consciousness. While I was riding him, he mirrored back his "is-ness" to me and for fleeting moments I saw the true reflection of no "I." It was like the emptying of my adulthood. The weight of my self-awareness dropped away, leaving me in the freedom of lightness and clarity. Once more I was experiencing the healing power of horses, that healing that comes through being just who they are and insisting that we be who we are, no masks, no ego. Ego is resistance to the fundamental truth of no separate identity. The ego, vehicle of the "I," has manifestations that are ugly. No-ego is beautiful and its manifestations are beautiful. Who we are is the sum of our manifestations, nothing more or less.

Later that week, I had a dream about Louis, that I left him in a field to fend for himself with just grass to eat and nothing else, and no company. I thought he would be all right and went off into a house, where I was searching for somewhere quiet to work but could not find anywhere peaceful enough. When I returned to him, he was sad and thin and lonely and not in good shape at all, so I hugged him and stroked him and communed with him; he nuzzled me, and I could feel that he was going to be all right after all and that I was going to look after him. When I woke up, with a feeling of sadness carved from my heart to my gut, I had the strange thought that Louis was my soul.

I was beginning to understand the mindfulness at the heart of riding, the interconnectedness on which it hinged, the softening and opening of the mind to accept and understand things just as they are, without interpretation, and obliterating any sense of separate identity. This is surely the experience of love, that love that encompasses equanimity and compassion, playfulness and selflessness. Where there is no resistance of the ego, there is transformation. Letting go of the resistance is the change. It is acceptance. Therein lies love and understanding.

To this day, I remember Louis with wistfulness bordering on heartache: The share never happened, because finally, after several rides and a few weeks later, it was clear that he was too wayward and powerful for a novice rider like me. Sometimes, Grace told me, it took two experienced people to hold onto him simply to take him from the stable to the paddock. This was the information that finally decided me. It would have been dangerous for both of us. I was also uncertain about Maureen: We lacked rapport. I felt that she tried to get her horses to do too much instead of letting it happen naturally. There was a prissiness and control about the way she ran the yard, and secretly I felt that she despised hacking out. Perfection in the ring was what she was after. I knew I would not be able to handle that. Much as I enjoyed messing around in the school, I did not take it that seriously, and I felt I would be permanently monitored. I certainly did not want to compete; I was doing it for myself and for the horse, not for outsiders to assess. On that subject I was clear. I was not going to use competition as a gauge of my riding. What mattered to me was being who I was and how that connected to my horse in the riding. But more than any of the other horses I rode during that time, Louis evokes grief in me, at the bereavement of the relationship I never had with this creature who was so needy of my love and care and affection. I mourn the times of fun and learning and companionship we never had. I would have loved to have gone nowhere with him and ridden him for the sake of riding him. I truly loved him. That black satin coat, those imploring eyes, that gentle soul, the untamed strength, and the beauty that was Louis.

TWENTY

no rule book

The anguished cry to my diary some weeks back still resonated in my mind, written in capitals: "Does anyone know of a stable run by Buddhists?" Like a seed it grew, and one day at the end of a yoga lesson it sprouted a shoot. I knew that my pupil, Isabel, had studied the Alexander Technique, and we were working with the principle of freeing the neck in order to release the back and deepen the breathing, when I threw in, "And this works when you are horseback riding too."

She picked up on it immediately.

"I didn't know that you were into riding."

"I took it up about 18 months ago," I told her, and began to relate some of my story to her.

"That's extraordinary," she said, "because my abiding passion is horses. I even wanted a career in riding before I started my family. I was brought up with it, and then when I was introduced to the Alexander Technique in my teens, it transformed everything. I found this fantastic riding teacher who works along Alexander lines both with the rider and with the horse. She's said to be the best in the country. In my opinion she is a genius, and watching her working with horses is something extraordinary. She knows them inside out and can do anything with them. She and her daughter still teach their pupils using the Alexander Technique. You must know them—they live just down the road from here."

"I don't think so," I said, interested. "What's her name?"

"It's Rona Jackson."

"No, I haven't come across her. Tell me about her."

"Well," said Isabel, "there is nobody, but nobody, who teaches like her. Anybody else is a waste of time if you are interested in riding this way. She understands the way that rider and horse reflect each other, and nothing escapes her attention. She lives her work, always has. She has a daughter, Caroline, who is one of my oldest friends, and she is an amazing teacher too. She studied with Nuno Oliveira . . ."

"Nuno Oliveira!" I gasped. "You mean she had dressage instruction under the greatest master this century?"

"Yes." Isabel smiled. "She lived out there for a while and was a regular pupil of his. And not only that, but Rona owns one of his horses."

"What?" I could hardly believe what I was hearing.

I was still recovering when Isabel delivered another *coup de foudre*.

"And she keeps him just a mile down the road here. At the farm stables at Little Brockham."

The next village down the road from me. Had I heard right? Still reeling, I heard Isabel say, "Look, I'll call Rona and Caroline and suggest that you might be interested in watching her teach. I'm sure she'd love for you to come—she will be very interested in you because you are a yoga teacher. She might even be able to give you a lesson sometime."

My feet didn't touch the ground for the rest of the day. That evening Isabel called to say that Rona had said it would be fine for me to watch a lesson; in fact, she would be delighted to meet me, and if I wanted to come to the stables the following Wednesday at noon I would be welcome.

I drove up a seemingly unending driveway to the farm under a steel gray sky etched with skeleton trees. Nothing moved in the intense cold. The narrow tarmac lane was lined on either side with high banks and fencing, over the top of which I could see cattle grazing the frozen pastures. It was at least a mile long, and I began to wonder whether I had found the right drive. I pulled up into the yard beside a gigantic barn and parked my car. There was nobody in sight, no vehicles, just silence. I got out, and as I closed the car door, two heads appeared over stable doors about 50 yards away, one chestnut and one gray. I walked toward them, held out a hand, and talked to them while I waited. Nobody came. I walked around to the entrance of the indoor school and peered inside: It was the size of an arena. Nobody there.

I waited another 10 minutes and was just about to give up when a little old Ford drove into the yard and parked opposite to mine. Out climbed a tiny woman who must have been in her 70s, wearing a woollen headscarf and Wellington boots. I could see a saddle on the back seat. She came to toward me smiling.

"You must be Ingrid!"

"Yes, hello. You must be Rona."

We shook hands. Rona Jackson came up to my shoulder. Her eyes continued to smile at me from her crinkly face as we made appropriate small talk, and then she made for the hay store and started to separate some bales of hay, still talking. She was wearing an old Barbour over a checkered woolen shirt and pants tucked into her boots. The headscarf stayed on. We connected immediately, talking about yoga, the Alexander

Technique, and riding. She was communicative and open, soft in her manner unlike so many of the horsey people I had been exposed to before. She was saying, ". . . and I always tell people to 'open the tunnel.'" Small talk was over.

"Open the tunnel?"

"Yes." She laughed. "To have a deep seat, to be down and re-laxed into the saddle, you want to open the tunnel. I know it sounds strange, but you'll understand, I know."

"I'll definitely try it next time I ride!" I said. I followed her to the stables.

Inside the first one stood a fine chestnut horse.

"This is Zhivago."

He stood in profile at the back of the stable against a brick wall, and what I saw was the classic conformation of a power-fully built stallion. This was a handsome and well-propor-tioned chestnut standing over 16 hands high, solidly built. His great barrel torso, gleaming red-gold, was supported by strong, firm legs and balanced by a well-muscled neck. His head was neat, with a little white patch on his nose. His light brown eyes were observing me, taking me in. He shook his chestnut mane with a soft blow of the nostrils.

"What a beautiful horse. Is he the one you got from Nuno Oliveira?"

"Yes. I got Zhivago just after Nuno died, and he was in a

dreadful state. He had been ridden by riders who didn't understand him, who used spurs on him, so he hated going into the school. He was really upset—not nervous or neurotic, just upset. His hindquarters had wasted because they had stopped training him properly. His rump was very thin and his hind legs set close together so they had lost the strength and balance that they now have. He just needed to be worked in the way that Nuno had worked him. I decided that I would rescue him and bring him around to where he had been before. The fact that he was originally trained by Nuno meant that it was all there, it just had to be brought out again. He's a good boy, really. Just a bit too much energy. He doesn't get ridden enough."

I had never seen anyone handle a stallion before. This was something different. You do not go up to stallions and cuddle them, not unless you want to risk life and limb. I wanted to offer my hand and stroke him, but he showed me his teeth, so I kept well back. I noticed how careful Rona was with him, even she who knew him so well. I was impressed and kept my distance. He had Russian blood in him, explained Rona, bred from the Don breed of horses that helped win the Napoleonic Wars—horses that are strong, tough fighters with spirit and stamina. I could just see him charging into battle. She went on to explain that Zhivago had to be kept in his stable most of the time because of the mares on the farm, and there was not room to make a safe paddock for him. Therefore, the pent-up energy mounted and he could be more than a handful.

"He's a dangerous horse if you don't know how to handle him."

I watched intrigued as she saddled and bridled him. By now her pupil, Kate, had arrived and was helping too. Together they led him out into the yard and around to the riding school. I found a chair on the side and sat to watch the lesson. Zhivago walked his first circle on the longe rein and my immediate impression was that he moved like a dancer. He appeared to float both in walk and in trot, and both gaits had the delicacy and precision of a superbly trained body. Once Rona had schooled him for a while, he released into his natural length. From a not-unnatural tightness, he warmed up into a long, graceful extended movement and went into a classic canter, his neck free, his impetus coming from the quarters. His tail arched and swished behind him to the rhythm of the canter. Then she began to bring him into a collected canter that looked like pictures out of the Spanish Riding School. This was a Nureyev among horses. After working him for a while in each direction, she called me over.

"Come and watch from where I am working," she said, so I joined her at the center of the circle and spent the next half-hour turning on a point like a whirling dervish to watch the work and dodge the rein. I watched fascinated as she instructed now Zhivago and then Kate, keeping my eyes on Kate too as she struggled to perfect her seat and hands to Rona's instructions.

I was so engrossed that I didn't notice Caroline arrive. She walked over to us and welcomed me with a broad smile. She was a pretty young woman with wavy blonde hair and peaches-and-cream skin. I liked her immediately. She was open, warm, talkative, funny, and obviously very bright. She welcomed me like an old friend, skipped the small talk and embarked on a monologue about beauty and harmony and how riding is an art form. Rona intercepted quietly, "You have to be a Yehudi Menuhin, you know. You are the artist with an instrument that creates beautiful things."

Caroline interrupted, "It's beyond analysis, of course, there's no A–Z of it, you can't teach by the rule book."

"Completely Zen then," I said. "It says in Zen that in life there are no rules; you make them up as you go along," and they both cried, "Yes!"

Here it all was, under my nose, on my doorstep. They spoke a language I could understand, and they likewise understood my language. Caroline turned to me and said, "It's such a difficult art, you see. You have to use this [pointing at her head], and this [pointing at her body]."

"Yes," I said, "and then do nothing."

"Exactly!" she said, laughing. We had tuned in. We were on the same wavelength. Caroline took over the teaching of Kate for the second half, while Rona corrected Zhivago on the longe. She taught beautifully, integrating Alexander work with skill and sensitivity. She was articulate and clear. I was impressed with what I saw.

I followed her out of the school at the end of the lesson and caught up with her as she fed the other horse, the beautiful gray with a massive head and hazel eyes. His name was Pushkin.

"Caroline," I said apprehensively, "would you consider giving me a lesson if you had a suitable horse for a beginner like me?"

"Oh, yes, of course," she said, "but we don't keep our other horses up here—I would give you a go on Zhivago."

Yet again I could hardly believe what I was hearing. Me, on a horse that had belonged to and been trained by Nuno Oliveira? Me? Was I waking or sleeping? I walked back to my car stunned. Next week, I would have a ride on Zhivago after Kate had finished her lesson and he was well-worked. I felt as if I had stumbled across the Holy Grail. Was my painful apprenticeship over?

TWENTY-ONE

noninterference

The following week I had a long phone call with Caroline. Our friendship blossomed quickly. I responded to her warmth, her bright brain, her openness and enthusiasm. She seemed genuinely interested in my work, in what I brought to the riding, and we discovered we had many interests in common, including being amateur painters. I told her how, the next time I rode Dulcie after meeting them, I had "opened my tunnel" and how it had instantly freed Dulcie up, how she had lengthened and loosened under me and how I too had relaxed. It had been like magic. I quizzed her about local teachers of the Alexander Technique. It was years since I had had Alexander instruction, and maybe now was the time to have some more.

"Ah! You don't know about Nicola?"

"No. Tell me about her."

"We swear by Nicola. We both go to her and so do most of our pupils. She rides Zhivago too, and has ridden for many years so she knows how to apply the Technique to horseback riding. Her work is fantastic, and you see the results in the riders immediately."

I decided to go and see Nicola before I sat on Zhivago, and made an appointment for the following Tuesday.

The work of the undersung genius F. M. Alexander hinges on what he called the psychophysical, the relationship between the body and the mind. On the premise that any physical activity involves the mind, Alexander stated that "you translate everything, whether physical, mental, or spiritual, into muscular tension." Thus, negative or positive states of mind will be reflected in the body. A horse, being finely tuned, if not hypersensitive, will pick up that tension, reflect it, and react to it, in instantaneous cause and effect. A calm, relaxed, and positive mind will be inherited by the horse, but so will nervousness and "trying too hard" on the part of the rider, a form of mental tension that transmits immediately.

The pioneering work of F. M. Alexander lay in his discovery of how we can learn to control our seemingly "automatic" reactions. His first breakthrough came in observing the vital relationship between head, neck, and back, how most of us misuse it, and how that impairs our natural functioning. He called this "primary control," because it is fundamental. For example, fear affects the neck muscles: The head is pulled back, the breath constricted, the larynx depressed, and the lumbar spine braced. Often these patterns become fixed. You can see them clearly in an anxious horse who will raise his head and hollow his back. Likewise, a tense human being will brace the neck, causing the lower back to tighten. If you free your neck, your head position aligns to its natural balance on top of the spine, and the back widens and lengthens. When a rider does this, the horse responds by reflecting the action, and coordination and balance follow naturally.

However, Alexander realized that we are dominated by our habits (he worked on himself and generalized his findings) and that our impulse is frequently to do the incorrect thing. Thus, thinking about it before we do it will prevent the wrong and facilitate the right. He called this pause—allowing time to think about an activity before it triggers a muscular response—"inhibition." This is a difficult new habit for fiery

Sagittarians sitting on the back of frisky horses to acquire, but I could see the point.

Then, having paused, you give yourself a conscious direction. His principle directions (which are mental directions rather than actually "doing it"—which can create more tension) are, "Let the neck be free so that the back can lengthen and widen, the head go forward and up, and the knees forward and away." Whether standing or sitting, going upstairs, getting out of a chair, walking down the street, or riding a horse, these directions free the body to a profound extent. A rider's attitude is mirrored in her body, and her mental directions affect the horse as much as her assumed posture.

Alexander advocated concentrating on the "means whereby" rather than focusing on goals—the latter he called "endgaining." In this, he was echoing a central insight of Zen, although he never studied it. Staying with the "now," with the present moment, leaves undisturbed the intrinsically natural balance of the bodymind. Undoubtedly the "how" of the journey determines the ultimate arrival, but if you pay attention to the process, to the now, the outcome will improve as a result—but not, paradoxically, because you had been focusing on it. It happens unintentionally. Employing the "means whereby" makes it possible to create constructive and open dialogue, whether on a horse or in everyday human situations.

What Alexander had discovered was a way of "nondoing," of noninterference with the intrinsic harmony of the body-mind that we experience so fleetingly and all too seldom in unintentional moments. The distinction between ends and means disappears and we rest in the eternal present. Our actions and thoughts are more and more likely to "slip like snow from a bamboo leaf" in natural accord with the laws of nature. He realized that we are all prisoners of our minds and bodies until, ironically, we realize that we are.

Over the next several weeks, I had regular Alexander Technique sessions with Nicola, and it began to transform the feel of my riding. She was a tiny, pretty woman running a busy practice in comfortable suburbia. Auburn-haired, soft spoken, and immaculately dressed, she guided me with her hands out of entrenched habits back to my original ease, leaving me feeling free, open, soft, and light. We talked endlessly about riding, about Zhivago, about Zen and yoga. We worked standing, sitting, getting out of a chair, and in the saddle. My diary of these weeks is full of her words:

The deepest musculature of the body is postural. It supports us. Let go of your outer peripheral muscles, which have sometimes distorted the posture. Return to the innocence of the original body.

*Lengthen from your sitz bones along the back of your thigh
bones when rising from a chair. Use this in the saddle, too. The
more you direct your knees forward, the more your spine moves up.*

Undo. Lengthen and widen.

*Your twist from right to left has locked your left hip and brought
your right shoulder forward. Your left side is slightly collapsed.
Open on the diagonal, from left hip to right shoulder. Practice this
lying down on the floor with your knees up, feet to the floor, and
then use it in your riding.*

*Feel the stirrups coming up to support you and think of resting
your feet in the stirrups. Think of your ankles as springs.*

*Remember that your spine ends in your face, at cheekbone level.
When you release your neck, this freedom goes right up into your
head. Keep your chin up, don't drop it. Open the front of your
spine, the front of your body.*

*Have soft wrists. Allow them to drop. Think of a spiral from
your elbow through your forearm, and release it. Be aware how the
slight twist in your body has also made your head tilt a little to the
right, so you have shortened your neck on that side.*

There was much more besides work for my body to absorb
and carry through awareness into practice. I was busy counting
the blessings that I had found all at the same time: an instructor
like Nicola, a superb horse like Zhivago, and teachers like the

Jacksons. The bitter gray cold of February failed to make me gloomy. The countryside seemed beautiful in all its moods.

The Alexander work took me back to the maxim that interfering with what is natural will always cause pain. He was in effect advocating wu-wei, noninterference, doing nothing. Inaction may turn out to be a genuine activity. It is not the inaction of sloth, indifference, sleepiness, but the inaction of a stillness that is attuned to its situation. It is the opposite of "trying," that effort that creates restless waves in the mind and interferes with natural harmony and balance. Never was this clearer to me than when I was riding; it was as if walls came up between me and the horse once I "tried," once my work became effortful. The horse picked it up immediately and tightened in response. One thing Rona said to me over the phone still rang in my ears: "The horse is the best teacher of all," reflecting my mistakes back to me in absolute honesty.

"A tree does not search for its fruits, it grows them," goes a Zen aphorism. The purpose of Zen is to see things as they are and to let everything go as it goes. It is not a way of assuming a mask with a designer label saying "Zen" on it. The instant that happens, you are likely to fall off, whether in riding or in the practice.

The essence of Zen is that things are entirely what they appear to be, and this underlines Goethe's plea, "Do not, I beg you, look for anything behind phenomena. They are themselves their own lesson." (This statement would appear to refute most "new age" mumbo jumbo in two sentences.) His was a profound insight, one that can be verified in the experience of noninterference, whether in bodywork à la Alexander, or in yoga, or on the back of a horse. To disturb something is to be attached to it. Thus, "the great way is not difficult": We make things difficult by complicating them, by interfering with what they are. Simplicity, the simplicity of stillness, is all. Paradoxically (again), it is that simplicity that usually is arrived at circuitously, but it was there all the time, innate, at the still point of our turning world, at the center of the dance.

TWENTY-TWO

forget all about bamboos

It was a bitterly cold day. It had snowed overnight, and the trees lining the roads were dusted with white, the wind freezing their twigs to a frozen sky. Birds were silent. The farmhouse pond was iced over except for a patch under the weeping willow. The paddocks lay numb, and when I walked across the yard the crisp top layer of the snow crunched under my boots. I watched Kate's lesson wrapped up in Zhivago's horse blanket to stop my bones from getting chilled. The indoor school was constructed of corrugated iron with a lofty roof, the windows just slatted with narrow boards and open to the elements. Chilling drafts swept over my anesthetized feet. Zhivago moved to Rona's commands on the longe, gradually lengthening his back and working from the quarters until his movements were connected and fluent. He obviously, touchingly, wanted to please her. I shivered into my huddle as I watched, desperately clinging to myself for warmth until the lesson was finished. Then it was my turn.

I carried the green plastic mounting block over to where he was standing and placed it beside him.

"Start getting on as soon as Kate gets off the other side," said Caroline, "otherwise Zhivago will think it's the end of his morning's work, and he'll want to get down and roll. Then we'll all be in trouble." She held Zhivago firmly as I mounted, swinging my right leg over the saddle.

"Nice," said Rona to Caroline approvingly. "I like the way she did that."

As I settled into the saddle, I felt as if I had melted around his back. In those first seconds, I felt something I had never experienced before. A horse in perfect balance, tone, togetherness, and symmetry. It felt natural, as if neither of us was there. I felt I had come home. The two were one. Zhivago's strong chestnut poll stretched in front of me, he flicked his ears and put them forward, and I reached over to stroke his neck. The lesson began.

Caroline adjusted my stirrups, advising me not to wear them as long as I had been used to. She placed my legs correctly underneath me and around Zhivago's ribs. She led us on the longe rein into the center of the school, and we started to walk a circle. I floated into Zhivago's graceful movement.

"Open the tunnel," said Caroline, "and ride in lightness. Never, ever, brace your back. Offer yourself to him, to his movement. Listen to him. Hear him."

As I "opened the tunnel," I felt my body lengthen and my trunk free upward. I freed my neck.

"Good," said Caroline, who could see this infinitesimal adjustment clearly. "Now 'invite' him. This will wake him up to you. Open the front of your body, and this opens him to you."

Yet again I experienced the miracle of cause and effect, of Zhivago knowing within a nanosecond what I was thinking and feeling. It was as if the opening of my posture opened up our consciousness, allowing us to connect without reservation. I breathed and felt him breathing. I felt his movement with total clarity. In that moment I was a beginner again. I knew that I knew nothing. I experienced it as it was, free of preconditions or expectations. The "as it was" was all I knew. Zhivago was so unlike any other previous experience that truly I would not have known what preconceptions or expectations to have. The force of it propelled me instantaneously into the present. Meanwhile my mind, childlike again in that instant, simply could not grasp the miracle of this special horse's allowing me to sit on his back.

As his walk lengthened and freed up under me, I only had to think "trot," literally, and forward he went into his floating movement, so easily that I went with him instead of the usual novice reaction of "braking," leaning back, and tightening. It was a beautiful, natural feeling. We started to work in sitting trot, a gait I had always found uncomfortable on other horses, finding it difficult not to bounce out of the saddle and land heavily back onto it. Zhivago's saddle, however, was a beautifully designed dressage saddle, and this contributed to the difference. But above all, his trot was so free and flowing that I felt I was riding on billowing silk. It reminded me of a factory I had visited in Varanasi where smiling Indians shook dozens of brilliantly colored saris out of their folds to make a sea of silk waves in the mirrored hall. I could relax into this smooth movement of Zhivago's trot immediately, with ease and comfort, and stay balanced in the saddle. Using the stirrups as my "ground," my legs so long that they felt as if they would touch the ground, and my ankles as springs, I could feel the wonderfully freeing direction of "forward and up."

The next time we went into rising trot, I only had to think it and it happened. He moved through me, and I stayed in perfect balance, not jerking backward or leaning forward. Again I went down into my feet as if they were roots going into the ground, and this had the effect of opening my hips so that they could just swing gently forward off the saddle and whisper back down again. As I lengthened from hip to knee and went down long into my heels, I felt as if my legs were floating. It was as if my body had become one from the heels to the head with nothing in between; it was effortless. It felt completely "right." I patted his silky neck to reward him as we finished, feeling his breathing and the warmth rising from his exercised body. The feeling of being one with Zhivago, of being totally present and focused, had obliterated time. Rona, genius teacher, saw what happened.

"All you have to do is to be," she smiled.

I was with someone whose insight I respected. My childlike trust of a potentially dangerous stallion and his owners allowed me the openness that comes from trust, and the spontaneity that did arise in freedom. This experience was giving a new meaning to spontaneity. The absence of underlying trust—in whatever situation—is paralyzing, so trust is an essential prerequisite of spontaneity. Fear, the fencing partner of trust, is the first thing that says "I," putting up walls around itself to protect the precious individuality that has no meaning in a world of interconnection. The child trusts, has no fear of either life or death until it is conditioned to have fear. "When body and mind achieve spontaneity, the Tao is reached and universal mind can be understood," says Lao-Tzu. Lack of spontaneity is characterized by deliberate effort, that insidious "trying too hard" that works the treadmill of duality.

There's a Zen instruction to draw bamboos for 10 years, become a bamboo, then forget all about bamboos when you are drawing. What it means is that you learn, you practice, you refine technique until you merge with your skill, and then you do not have to think consciously about it any more. It has been integrated into your consciousness. You empty yourself, you let go of it all, and move beyond technique to soul. In riding, this means you feel above all, and you ride with this feeling, this soul.

I drove home from the lesson in a dream, knowing that I had been in the hands of magicians. I scribbled down notes as soon as I arrived back. They are incoherent with joy. "Sublime horse, so so wonderful. Difficult to describe. Merged with him. Peak experience. Heaven. I think I went to Heaven."

TWENTY-THREE

knowing is the way of fools

"A god alone can hold this sense of oneness," said Mephistopheles to Faust (Goethe gave him many of the best lines). That first ride on Zhivago was an out-of-the-ordinary experience whose memory remains clear in every detail and feeling, but I could not hope to repeat it intentionally. There is a saying in Zen, rapping incipient hubris on the head, "After the ecstasy, the laundry." Newly enlightened monks were told to go and wash the dishes, not in any spirit of penance but in the realization that washing the dishes is enlightenment like any other everyday activity, if we are enlightened. Thus, I sensed that I must allow the experience to integrate without clinging to it and expecting it to happen every time I rode. In some sense, I could never be the same again anyway, so I could let go of any concept of a pinnacle reached, and simply accept that the moment of ultimate realization was a clarification of the utmost simplicity that would affect my life whatever happened. Never did the Zen aphorism make more sense than now: "You cannot get it by taking thought; you cannot reach it by not taking thought."

The subsequent lessons with Caroline over the following weeks took me to new yet familiar places, to where I had longed to be. Zhivago was the teacher above all, even in simple sessions of walking and trotting on the longe. We spent time walking without stirrups: Caroline commanded, "Empty! Empty the legs, the body, the mind! Only then can the mind come into oneness with the horse."

"You are an artist," she said to me, "so you will understand. It is all about feel. That above all. It is not about thinking."

Working with the Alexander direction of knees forward, lengthening along the back of the thighbone from the sitz bones, my seat deepened. I began to open my front and widen my back and to improve the chin-sternum relationship. Letting down in the hips, I allowed my feet to rest even deeper in the stirrups. Caroline gave me an image for the transition down from rising trot to sitting trot: "Be like thistledown," she said, and this worked magically in lightness and balance.

We rested after a long trotting session, and Caroline adjusted my legs so that my thighs spiraled inward, my inner calves ready to lightly tell Zhivago to move, my feet straight and heels long. "Open the ankles," she said. This was an enlightening instruction. Zhivago proceeded to give me inimitable glimpses of freedom and length, instants of togetherness where I realized the truth that all that mattered was being who I was and leaving him to be what he was.

"Think of having three gears," she said. "Just as if you were driving a car. When you are upright, you are in neutral. If you arch your back slightly and take your heels down, this is your 'stop' gear, your brake; and when you want to go, the shoulders move forward slightly. You still need to let go of your legs; you are holding on to them in the hips. Imagine them touching the ground, and this will release them from the pelvis. Open the groin too—imagine that you have eyes there and that you are opening them!"

Absorbing this instruction, at the same time as "opening my tunnel," I felt loose, light, and free on Zhivago's back. I allowed him his movement by not interfering, but the moment I tightened, he responded with tension, reflecting it back to me with a clarity that my body understood instantly. It was clear that my seat needed a lot of work.

"But your upper body work is excellent," said Caroline. "Your head-neck-back configuration is great, due no doubt to all those years of yoga! Your hands are OK, but you need to teach him to love your hands, to love the bit by making it feel friendly and comfortable. Talk to him through your hands. He's a brilliant horse, and he will understand what you're saying."

In these lessons, she taught me to ride with shorter stirrups so that I could feel my feet in them as if they were on the ground: "The stirrups are your ground." She repeated endlessly the need for noninterference, because of my propensity to do too much.

"Then open the shoulders, open the tunnel, free the neck, and keep soft hands—and that's all you need to do." We both laughed. "That's all . . ."

"Well done," said Rona, who had rejoined us. "You are doing really well. And now make space between your back teeth—which is another way of saying relax the jaw—and you'll find how much difference that makes to the freedom of your neck and back. Stillness and peace are at the core of great riding. If you look at pictures of Nuno Oliveira, you can see this in his seat."

My diary records their wise words:

You must be supple and flexible, upright and deep. An elastic back is essential for lightness and collection. Keep both long and wide in the torso.

Remain independent of whatever happens so that you stay in balance, yet remaining—of course—interdependent. This requires understanding. You learn to control yourself before you can control the horse.

The calmness that should be found in activity itself, according to Zen, seemed to be exactly how Rona was describing Nuno Oliveira's riding. Also according to Zen, the sincerity of an undivided mind that does not dither between alternatives is the essential quality of naturalness. This was my experience on horseback, and most especially on Zhivago: Noninterference, focus, and simplicity were prerequisites of riding him in balance and harmony. I was still learning to let go, learning not to interfere, not to fear, learning to do and not to do. "One is what one does": The mirror was still held up, as it always was and always would be. The learning was in every moment, yet I would never know anything beyond the knowledge of the moment. The art of riding, like the art of life, is undoubtedly an art that is never finished. It is never the same twice. The "don't know" mind of Zen, the wisdom of not knowing, kept the door open to limitless learning without providing any answers.

One consolation of not knowing is the assurance in Zen that foolishness is one of the paths to wisdom. However inept (or skilled) I was in my riding, however inadequate (or adequate even), there was a possibility to learn. Maybe to understand. Yet also to know that the most dangerous thing in the world, according to Zen, is to think that you understand something. "Knowing is the way of fools." Among its most attractive aspects is the Zen tradition of nourishing self-effacement and modesty, because the practice blends into everyday life so as to pass almost unnoticed, and the more it is practiced the more ordinary it becomes.

"The only wisdom we can hope to acquire," says T. S. Eliot, "is the wisdom of humility. Humility is endless." The awakened mind of Zen is ordinary, it is nothing special. The real miracles of life are that when I feel hungry I eat, and when I feel thirsty I drink. Awakening is something natural, not remote, not forced. It is here and now, in this moment. It may be triggered by something that is startlingly obvious. And above all, it is simple: If there is difficulty around it, it is missing the point.

Zen depreciates the ego, it deprecates self-conscious virtue, honoring rather the intuitive insight that arises from the integrity of a whole and balanced being, whose manifestation is a harmonious relationship between the inner and the outer world. The cultivation of the inner life is reflected in full engagement with physical existence, because Zen meets the paradox of duality by confronting it directly. What a relief this is, not to withdraw into concepts and dogmas but simply to engage spontaneously and fully in the miracle of life.

TWENTY-FOUR

rivers and mountains

Spring came early that year. Its beauty reinforced in me the understanding of the transforming power of the present moment. As my beloved Henry Miller wrote, "It's not in the hereafter that things may be realized, but now." So seldom do we taste the fullness of the present. The horses I had ridden had taught me how the instant is forever, the single moment eternity, how the now is the only direct experience we have, ever. The paradox is that if we lose ourselves in that present, when we forget ourselves as in those timeless moments I had had on Dulcie, Jade, Leo, Zhivago, and the others, that is when we are most fully present. It is then that difficulties cease to exist, it is then that we enjoy life richly, to its brim. The present moment becomes the central pivot of aliveness, never still yet unmoving, moving in stillness, impossible to define or locate, but nevertheless an undeniable experience.

This condition of simple clarity requires unlearning over learning. Knowing that there is nothing to know (and to lament that it is so difficult to communicate this "nothing to know" to others), this is one of the deepest experiences in the world. How simple, how unpretentious. Zen does not attempt to transcend anything—it remains grounded in direct experience. Henry Miller saw it this way: "The sole meaning, purpose, intention . . . my dears, is not to understand Life, or to mold it, or change it, or even to love it, but to drink of its undying essence . . . for there is only the marvelous and nothing but the marvelous."

The way is knowing and not knowing, it is and is not. This is the art of the mystic who is not mystical, who travels in the ordinary world knowing the ordinary to be the most extraordinary and elusive. Thus, "Those who know cannot explain, and those who explain do not know." Miller, unselfconsciously echoing Zen, said that the only real answer to any fundamental question is experience itself, adding, "I believe that chance does not exist in the universe, everything follows rules. Life has great significance. If you haven't absorbed that fact, it's not worth a thing, not worth speaking about. The important thing is that man should never lose sight of his link with the universe. Life is a miracle. For me, everything is mystery and miracle."

Nature makes everything as it should be: Nothing needs to understand why it is as it is. So if we obey our own nature, we will walk freely and undisturbed. If we let go, trust, and stay with the eternal present, in full awareness, then

> *Less and less is done*
> *Until nonaction is achieved*
> *When nothing is done, nothing is left undone.*
> —Tao-te Ching

How true this is of riding too: the method of no method, the soul beyond the technique. The fundamental paradox is that any form of harmony is not achieved by trying to achieve it, but rather by not trying to achieve anything, by ridding oneself of desire. Thus the Zen master is not pushed around by the passions and currents of society; he or she has a clear, serene view of reality grounded in experience of the ordinary, knowing that the answer is in the question, the resolution in the paradox, the end in the beginning.

I had reached a quiet place in my riding now, as if the imperative for urgent searching had abated. Perhaps it had something to do with this perception. A shift had taken place in my personal dilemma too, a recognition that the reality of a relationship can never happen with a mask, a mask that masked a hollow place but had failed to hide it. To resolve the situation, having at last accepted it with some degree of equilibrium, I could see a way of divergence that was kind, nondestructive—and possibly even creative. This, whatever risk it entailed, would be the way ahead.

"No matter what you touch and you wish to know about, you end up in a sea of mystery. You see there's no beginning and no end, you can go back as far as you want, forward as far as you want, but you never get to it, it's like the essence." This is Henry Miller; he, Eliot, Dōgen, and many other great souls are like those mythological heroes who complete the journey of their quest by finally returning to the place where they began. The end is the beginning, the beginning also an ending. Clarification was always there, under our noses, but we had to look somewhere else in order to find it. And it is the ordinary that contains the answer. A Zen master said, "Before practicing Zen, rivers were rivers and mountains were mountains. When I practiced Zen, I saw that rivers were no longer rivers and mountains no longer mountains. Now I see that rivers are again rivers and mountains are again mountains." The April sunshine lit horse-chestnut buds outside my study window.

Finding is, paradoxically, the process of losing so that the ordinary can be discovered. The search continues until the beginning is found, and the place recognized and known for the first time. This experience happens in complete simplicity, unintentionally, whether riding a horse, looking in awe at a rose window in Chartres, listening to a Bach cello suite, gazing at an oak in autumn color, or walking down a street in New York. It costs the struggling psyche practically everything as it collapses its redundant structures and reconstitutes itself in the clarity of its original home.

TWENTY-FIVE

endings and beginnings

Nothing happens next. This is it," said the Zen monk to the novice as they sat in zazen. Maybe there is no destination, unless it is a new way of looking at things. My first hack across the English countryside at harvest time under the sign of Virgo nearly 2 years before, when horses had seemed to me aliens from another universe, had opened up new perspectives for me, coinciding (by what synchronicity I cannot know) with my introduction to Zen. My starting point had been unfocused fear, but now I know that there is only one fear and that all fears are the same. So although in all honesty there was no end to the ultimate fear of death or terrible injury, I was no longer frightened by the horses themselves as I grew to understand them; indeed, it now seems inconceivable that I had been so scared of such sensitive and gentle creatures. How could I have been so terrified? The answer may be that since a horse's main instinct is fear, it mirrored my own instinctive fears, but because these were now based on a clearer understanding of the unpredictable and high-strung equine nature they had lost some of their grip. Certainly now, weighed on the scales against the joy, the freedom, the activity, the understanding, the love that horseback riding had brought to me, there was no doubt which side came down heavier.

A choice always remained, after all: a choice to continue riding or not, to dice with death or not. I tended to come down on the side of Miller: "The more fully we embrace our lives, *live* our lives, the easier it is to accept the notion of death. The main thing is not to fear." In the last analysis, who knows anything about death? Nobody. After millennia of thinking about it, not even the greatest minds have come any closer to answering the perennial question of "what happens next?" that so chills the soul. So why bother about it? Why not use our consciousness of the awesome and sometimes dreadful mystery of mortality to drink every drop from the goblet of life while it is still in our hands?

Almost fearless now, I could celebrate the love and respect I had found in myself for the animal more closely involved in the process of human civilization than any other. Often, passing horses grazing in a field, I would stop and gaze, commune and talk with them as I stroked an offered muzzle. Even though I had not become the hero of my hero and conquered my fears completely, I was now more alive to the "security of insecurity" and the wisdom of not knowing than I had been before I started riding. I could openly embrace risk in more than one area of my life. My higher self wholeheartedly agreed with Miller: "The worst is not death, but being blind, blind to the fact that everything about life is in the nature of the miraculous."

One morning in high summer, I took Dulcie out on my own. A rooster was crowing in the far field as I walked across the paddock, and she gave a whinny of recognition as she looked up from her grazing, ears pricked forward. A soft blow through her nostrils and she took the offered carrot as I slung a halter over her neck. She walked languidly behind me as I led her to the gate to be tacked up, lifting her hooves rhythmically over the long grass, her blaze nodding at my shoulder. She dropped her head to tear at some luscious new grass and I smelled her sweet smell in the freshness of the new day.

We rode along grassy lanes beside mature hedgerows lush with flowering yarrow, white wild sweet pea, mist blue scabious, and the gall of the dog-rose. Viburnum in flower was attracting clouds of butterflies. Wheat was ripe in the fields under the sweltering July sky. Dulcie cantered hell-for-leather across a vast acreage of fallow ground, her spirits high: She was full of the joys of summer that day, fit, eager, and forward going. We tore across open fields, the hot wind pouring past my face under my riding hat, her heavy iron hooves thudding over the cracking ground, crunching the cut straw. Taking a grassy track down the hill into the village, we stood outside my cottage to rest, perspiring and panting in the torrid heat, before returning at a gallop up the hill and across the open field again, retracing our steps in less than half the time. I slowed her into a steady trot, bouncing gently in the saddle in sitting trot as we slowed to a walk and caught our breath again.

The feeling of that ride was of confidence, a comfortable confidence that I could not have dreamed of in those first fearful days of awkwardness and ignorance. Breathless, I felt fully alive and aware, ready to cope with anything unexpected. We walked to the crest of the hill where we could see open countryside in all directions: East Anglia in the dog days of midsummer with its rolling wheatfields and circling birds. Pausing to look around, I inhaled pure happiness. My great teacher's words echoed in my mind: "Let each one turn his gaze inward and regard himself with awe and wonder, with mystery and reverence; let each one promulgate his own laws, his own theories; let each one work his own influence, his own havoc, his own miracles."

But something did happen next. I became ill and for nearly a year was unable to ride at all. At first I refused to admit defeat and forced my body into things it was unable to cope with. Gradually it became clear that the illness would triumph over my will to continue and that any riding I could do in the future would be severely limited due to the permanent disability that was the legacy of the disease. The privilege of regular practice, of those special relationships I had had with "my" horses, these were now denied me, and as I watched people ride past my cottage on their beloved horses I felt achingly sad. It seemed that the door that had opened for me into the secret places where horses live was closing inexorably.

The illness hit me in winter, and through that summer I was pushing myself against currents of fatigue and an undertow of low energy. I decided to take myself to a remote Greek island to rest and recharge awhile. Flying into the mainland airport, I experienced the horrors of its overcrowded chaos before driving through the bustling streets of the city to the harbor where the ferry was waiting. I stood for most of the journey leaning over the rail staring at the sea, hypnotized by the waves breaking rhythmically away from the boat as it plowed through the water. They danced and reveled under my gaze, the playful foam dissolving endlessly, frothing and disappearing into the blue water, only to reappear and dance again. Insubstantial white bubbles vanishing back into the waves after their dance was done. Just like us. Like dreamers, we look into mirrors and we dream, and dreams arise and die like waves breaking over each other, returning to the element from which they come.

In the light of such understanding, the regrets and disillusionments of my illness began to disperse. One dream might have died, but another would be reborn. My life, after all, could never be the same again now that it had been touched so deeply by Equus. I had learned that endings are beginnings, and all the steps forward I would take in my life would contain the magic of that experience that I had translated for myself as the Zen of horseback riding. Most of all, I took with me the treasure of experiencing the richness of the present moment, that container of past and future, and knowing that that is all there is. Yet it was unwillingly and with a sad heart that I left the wonderland where I had experienced so many joys and fears and closed the looking glass door behind me.

postscript

There once was a snake who thought he had legs. When he tried to walk, he found that he couldn't move. What to do? He thought long and hard about the problem until he realized that he did not have legs after all. Then he moved easily and freely across the land.

Writing about Zen is as self-contradictory as putting legs on the snake. Zen is skeptical about words and systems, so a book about Zen has a poor provenance. Dōgen said, "You should stop searching for phrases and chasing after words. Take the backward step and turn the light inward." Duly admonished, the author humbly defers to this wisdom, but nonetheless seeks to justify the experience of attempting to match words to experience. There is a Zenrin poem that goes:

postscript

You cannot get it by taking thought:
You cannot get it by not taking thought.

Since we convey both thoughts and experiences by means of language, herein lies a challenge to convey thoughts through the expression of thoughts. This ability is after all what separates humans from other creatures. Such an expression may well fall short, but its very folly may be—in the best Zen tradition—the justification.

"The instant you speak about something, you miss the mark," goes a Zen saying. Although it is not based on words and concepts, Zen famously manipulates words and concepts (in koans*) in order to reveal the reality that transcends them—one of the characteristic paradoxes intrinsic to its tradition. There may well be a gulf between the experience and the description, which is why the Buddha frowned on describing ultimate reality that can only be about direct spiritual experience. Yet would civilization not be poorer without Dōgen, Bashō, Seng-ts'an, Ryōkan, Alan Watts, Lao-Tzu, Chuang-tzu, and the other Zen masters quoted in these pages, let alone the huge heart of Henry Miller, and the poetry of

* A koan is a paradoxical question—a kind of riddle—containing in its answer the principle of eternal truth.

T. S. Eliot, who engaged in his "intolerable wrestle with words and meanings"?

> *Words strain,*
> *Crack and sometimes break, under the burden,*
> *Under the tension, slip, slide, perish,*
> *Decay with imprecision . . .*

and yet they are worth struggling with, sometimes, for

> *Words, after speech, reach*
> *Into the silence.*

A book about Zen cannot be a book about Zen yet is, paradoxically to the last, a book about Zen.

"Words!" cried Seng-ts'an. "The Way is beyond language.'"

> *How refreshing, the whinny of a pack horse*
> *Unloaded of everything.*
>
> —Zen saying

HENRY MILLER

There are few people we meet during our lifetimes who make a deep and lasting impact on us. When I read *The Colossus of Maroussi* in Greece, more years ago than I care to count, I recognized that a special soul had come into my life. His name is Henry Miller. I have devoured almost everything he has written (and that's a lot). I couldn't put him down. His often outrageous directness, his enthusiasm and joy, his humor and sincerity, his paradoxical innocence, disarmed me. How many men, at 80, could write with his energy, blasting people out of their mental bomb shelters and having fun while he spread joy and confusion? Here is a great man who celebrates his own innate insecurity; who understands the meaning of acceptance, of humility, of surrender; who is never afraid to be naked and vulnerable; and whose sense of wonder is his religion. He is forever transgressing boundaries. No "isms" or ideologies for him, just huge, generous openheartedness that embraces life with its light and shadow, glory and squalor. His wisdom is unpretentious, grounded in the world of his experience, funny and imbued with a sense of the marvelous. For me he is an Olympian figure, a prose poet of the ordinary, a mystic and a man of clay, a Master.

HENRY MILLER, born Brooklyn, New York, 1891
died California, 1980

HENRY MILLER BOOK LIST

A short list of some of my favorites. Many of them are out of print but obtainable secondhand via the Internet. The principal two publishers are New Directions and Grove/Atlantic.

Big Sur and the Oranges of Hieronymus Bosch
The Colossus of Maroussi
Sexus, Plexus, Nexus
Black Spring
Sextet: Six Essays
My Life and Times
The Books in My Life
A Literate Passion (letters with Anaïs Nin)
Reflections
The Cosmological Eye
Henry Miller on Writing
Nothing but the Marvelous (anthology)

A LITTLE ZEN BACKGROUND

The practice of Zen arose in the 6th century when Indian Buddhism met Taoism in China. Zen merged speculative elements of these traditions with the practical, the metaphysical with the down-to-earth. It was called Ch'an, and it stressed meditation as the way to realize the Buddha mind. It reached its golden age in the T'ang and Sung dynasties (7th to 12th centuries) and arrived in Japan, where around 1,190 schools of Sōtō Shū and Rinzai-shū still flourish today. The first Zen teachers came to the West around 1905.

CHUANG-TZU

Chuang-tzu was born in China and died an old man in 310 B.C. He was a traveling freelance philosopher who wrote on Taoism which, rather than being a set of doctrines or beliefs, is an attitude, a "way"—a way of seeing and of living. Its followers, instead of wanting to satisfy transient wants and needs, are content to accept what life offers without wishing it to be otherwise. They tend to acquire great skills and artistry, but without self-consciousness, pride, or ambition. Chuang-tzu's reputation and writings spread rapidly across China, and *The Book of Chuang-tzu*, his collected wisdom and wit, has been in circulation ever since.

SENG-TS'AN

Seng-ts'an (died 600), whose name means "the glory of the monks," became enlightened when he understood that the Buddha (awakening), the dharma (the way of understanding and compassion) and the sangha (the purity of the monastic order) were not different from the mind. He taught that the mind is universal and undifferentiated, that it is itself the only reality. He went on to become the Third Zen Patriarch in succession to Hui-k'o, the Second, and Bodhidharma, the First, the monk who originally brought Indian Buddhism to China.

HUI-NENG

Hui-neng (638–713) is a central figure of Zen Buddhism, the last of the Grand Masters and founder-teachers of Zen. Originally an illiterate woodcutter, he attained enlightenment as a young man and went on to teach direct insight into the nature of awareness. He lived during the T'ang dynasty (619–906) at a time when both Chinese culture and Chinese Buddhism were flourishing under imperial patronage. His simple, down-to-earth teachings on how to transcend the ordinary and awaken to the "way" reached countless followers, and his wonderfully readable sutras (teachings) are still in print today.

DŌGEN

Dōgen was born in Kyoto, Japan, in 1200 and became one of the most significant thinkers in Japanese religious history. After training as a monk, he traveled around China for 4 years before returning to his native country to teach and write. His colossal *Shōbōgenzō* was not published until 500 years after his death. He reconciled Zen with the greater traditions of Buddhism, and threw light—by means of explicit illustrations—on the logical procedures of Zen koan meditation, the way to experiencing truth directly. He exploded the myth that Zen awakening is an irrational process. He believed that practicing and enlightenment, process and goal, are inseparable. He was granted a "Great Master" title of honor by the emperor of Japan.

BASHŌ

Bashō lived from 1644 to 1694. He is thought by the Japanese to be their finest haiku poet (a haiku is a poem of 17 syllables, although this is often lost in translation, of which the first and last lines are five syllables). Bashō experienced satori (enlight-enment) under his master, Butcho, and the resulting haiku remains one of his best known:

Old pond
Leap-splash—a frog